Art 4–11:

Art in the early years of schooling

Edited by **Margaret Morgan**
in association with Suffolk County Council

STANLEY
THORNES

First Published in 1988 by
Basil Blackwell Limited
Reprinted 1989 (twice), 1990

Reprinted in 1991 by
Simon & Schuster Education
Reprinted 1992, 1994

Reprinted in 1995 by
Stanley Thornes (Publishers) Ltd
Ellenborough House
Wellington Street
CHELTENHAM GL50 1YD
England

A catalogue record for this book is available from the British Library.

ISBN 0 7487 2311 0

Cover illustration by Melanie Russell and Selina Trenter (aged 9)

Designed by Bob Prescott Design Associates, Oxford.

Typeset in Great Britain
by Columns, Reading

Printed in Hong Kong by Wing King Tong Co., Ltd.

Contents

Preface

THIS PUBLICATION is based on the *Suffolk County Guidelines: 4–11 years* first published in 1985. It has been considerably edited, updated, and expanded in some sections.

It is the result of the work of a group of teachers who met with the County Art Adviser initially over the period of two years. Their self-chosen brief was to produce some form of guideline for practice for teachers of pupils of 4–11 years. They believed that there was an urgent need for some form of guidance which would enable a structured and balanced art experience, supported as fully as possible by information of a practical nature.

We hope that the relevance of the book will be apparent to teacher trainers and trainees, headteachers, members of staff and interested parents whether they consider themselves well informed or lacking in expertise and confidence in this wonderful experience we call art.

Dedication

To Robin Tanner

'You see, my belief is this, that the arts above all other activities involve us in that subtle exercise of choice. They demand discrimination, and choice demands rejection. Every creative act is an act of choosing. When I look at these paintings and all this work here and I realise how much choosing, selection, has gone on in the minds of those children – do I put this down or that? – do I place this here or there? – And I think we are all given this wonderful power and we are given this power to respect all kinds of material – human material, paper, cloth, wood, everything. . . .'

(1984) Excerpt from a talk given by Robin Tanner, H.M.I., teacher and artist, who has done so much in his lifetime to influence the direction of Primary Education.

Working party members

Margaret Adams	Margaret Riches
Pauline Bebbington	Anna Roberts
Margaret Bidmade	Fred Sedgwick
Gwen Bryson	Ann Taylor
Eddie Casey	Tina Webber
Margaret Morgan	Tim Wilson
June Pendle	Michael Woods

Assisted by

Madeleine Addyman	Pauline Lockyer
Di Brendish	Paul Marshall
Mary Bolton	Robin Massey
Anne Cole	Helen Revell
Joan Crowson	Kathleen Rowe
Di Gooding	Eileen Rowe
Irene Edwards	Janet Swann
Kevin Keating	Angela Walkiden
Margaret Knights	Gillian Walsh
June Leslie	John Wilkinson
Germaine Lismore	

Acknowledgements

Thanks are due to Doreen Hindle, Philippa Thorpe and Michael Woods for use of material from dissertations and special studies, and to the staff and pupils of Suffolk Schools whose projects and work have been used in this publication.

To John Bowden, Bob Clement and Rod Taylor for permission to use extracts from their publications, and Alexandra Fairman for the use of her project.

To photographers: Peter Clapham, Trevor James (Suffolk County Council photographer)
Steve Wolfendon
Diss Evening News

To Malcolm Annandale and Westbourne High School pupils for some of the diagrams.

To John Wilkinson for the 'Handwriting' extracts.

Thanks are due to the following schools for contributing to projects in this publication:

Albert Pye Primary School, Bacton Middle School, Beyton Middle School, Bramford Primary School, Downing Primary School, Grange Primary School, Guildhall Feoffment Primary School, Gisleham Middle School, Hadleigh County Primary School, Hartest Primary School, Helmingham Primary School, Ixworth Middle School, St Helen's Primary School, Kingston Middle School, Kirkley Middle School, Mellis Primary School, Nacton Primary School, Occold Primary School, Palgrave Primary School, Raeburn Primary School, Stoke Ash Primary School, Trimley St Mary Primary School, Tudor Road Primary School, Wetheringsett Primary School.

Introduction

ART IS A unique form of experience which cannot be imitated in any other way. It is not only non-verbal, it is *pre*-verbal and since all human beings – unless suffering from some forms of handicap – gain a large proportion of their experience and understanding through sight and touch, it is very much a part of our educational grounding and potential.

Art experience is deeply imbedded in the realm of life skills for all children, not only the gifted or less able. Joyful response, the ability and confidence to create and bring practical and theoretical skills to bear on a variety of problems, to assess the potential of ideas, tools and materials, will have consequences far beyond the discipline itself. Confidence in the value of intuitive as well as logical modes of thinking, supported by practical experience in developing and refining ideas, will spill over into many parts of children's lives and stand them in good stead as adults.

It is a matter of some urgency that we look at the philosophy, curriculum and practice we offer in art in our schools. We know from a wide variety of research projects that the early years are formative years and in fact foundation for life in art experience will end, for some children, at 13 years of age. What will they have gained in understanding in the seven or eight years course we offer in the primary years of schooling? What kind of a foundation have we laid for those pupils who do follow an art option, and possibly a later career in art and design? Have we given them appropriate vision, insight, and skill? It may well depend on the potential we introduced them to, or perhaps failed to, which influenced later decisions.

If we genuinely believe in the need to develop the 'whole person' and to offer a balanced education, taking into account mind, body and spirit, we must assure ourselves that sufficient energy, time, resources and expertise are available for art and craft in all our schools. It is crucially important that as teachers, we have the vision to see our own and the child's art experience as an ever-changing and developing mode of human response and initiative, unique in its relationship to education.

Experience comes to us through our senses – sight, hearing, touch, taste and smell, together with subtler forms of awareness which as yet we find hard to define. A major question we need to ask ourselves is how far do we consciously extend the children's skills in experiencing? Looking and really seeing? Listening and hearing? Touching and understanding?

Through vision we take in much information from our environment in the natural world and in manmade form, we respond, we feel emotionally, we learn. Fine art and craft, photography, film and television, advertisement, the printed page, all offer us information and experience as well as a great deal of pleasure and enjoyment. Through sound we learn more of the nature of things, find mood suggested and sometimes colour and pattern, enjoy rhythm, harmony and sequence. Through touch and movement we experience qualities, learn more of the nature and characteristics of things and begin to understand form and space. Through taste and smell we build up a complete picture of our world. These senses offer us joys and discriminatory possibilities peculiar to themselves, enriching our experiences of mood and memory.

The education we offer our children should never be haphazard. We have a responsibility to plan a curriculum structure which accepts every child as he is and enables him to develop his experience and potential as far as is humanly possible.

The following passages from *The Arts in Schools* are of interest in this context:

'Living in the present
To see education only as a preparation for something that happens later risks overlooking the needs and opportunities of the moment. Children do not hatch into adults after a secluded incubation at school. They are living their lives now. Helping them towards an independent and worthwhile life in the adult world of the future pre-supposes helping them to make sense of and deal with the experiences which they suffer or enjoy in the present. The roles they adopt later and the employment they will seek will partly depend on what they become as individuals – what capacities and capabilities are developed or neglected – during the formative years of education. It follows that schools should enrich and broaden children's experiences through a broad and balanced curriculum. Literacy and numeracy are an important part of education. They should not be mistaken for the whole of it . . . .'

'Society needs and values more than academic abilities. Children and young people have much more to offer. The arts exemplify some of these other capacities – of intuition, creativity, sensibility and practical skills. We maintain that an education in these is quite as important for all children as an education of the more academic kind and that not to have this is to stunt and distort growth as intelligent, feeling and capable individuals.'

(*The Arts in Schools* Calouste Gulbenkian Foundation 1982)

Our major aim as teachers must surely be to offer our children a rich, broad based developmental pattern of education. It is important to take into account fully the stage the child has reached and to see them for what they are – unique human beings with a mixture of gifts, difficulties and potential. Children living in the world of today face incessant change, where values, ways of working and lifestyle require constant re-appraisal, and where they may well need to learn many different skills and approaches. Flexibility of thought, the ability to work in different ways with people of different backgrounds and cultures, tolerance, perseverance and independent initiative will be some of the qualities and skills which will stand children in good stead in any situations they may need to face in later life.

The need to foster emotional stability based on a sensitive understanding of themselves and their own reactions, and on other people's, can be seen to be a crucial, integral part of this 'whole' education.

Literacy, numeracy and graphicacy (mark making in all its forms) can arguably be seen as a three legged structure supporting all symbol systems, but it is the last which is the young child's major system in early years and the one from which the other two grow. Each of the systems has a unique part to play and should be mutually supportive in the development of the whole person.

Graphicacy, together with its three-dimensional counterpart, the ability to make forms, also precedes the other systems in man's early history. Each system was evolved in response to man's needs within the world in which he was living.

Education in the first years of schooling is not rigidly defined by subject areas and the fact that most children are being taught by one teacher, or a comparatively small number of teachers, allows for a rounded view of an individual's experience. Flexibility in balancing time between various activities over the period of a week or term is a possibility.

The inherent dangers in this system pertain to the teacher's confidence and experience in handling all areas of the curriculum. Many teachers feel that they have no flair for, or understanding of, art and thus they may offer children a lightweight experience which fails to extend or stimulate them.

Sound art, craft and design education requires insight into the nature of art experience, and understanding of the development of the children, their visual and tactile imagery, and the qualities and potential of materials. On this knowledge and basis we believe that it is appropriate to build a structure for a flexible developmental programme for the first years of schooling.

Part One

The nature of art in the first years of schooling

Introduction

SOME AMERICAN Indian tribes do not have a word in their vocabulary for 'art', yet their cultures overflow with paintings, drawings, sculpture, and models, weaving, pattern-making and decoration. It is so much a part of their life needs and style that it seems to become as unselfconscious as breathing. There would appear to be a close analogy with this and the way young children move naturally into art and design experiences, where the need for the experience comes first, and only at a later stage, if necessary, are descriptive words attached to them.

Very young children are moved to play, experiment with and rearrange the materials of their world. This stage is of the greatest importance, as they are building up understanding of the way in which materials and media behave. During this time they become aware of what is happening and of the significance of cause and effect. They seldom show interest in what has been done after they have finished working. They may well enjoy the activity for the feel of the materials or for the movements they are making.

As time goes on children become more confident. They begin to control and organise the material into patterns, structures and forms, although at times they may destroy what has been done as a part of the process of experiment or in anger or frustration. They enjoy the tactile qualities of materials – sand, mud, water, clay, plasticine, fabrics and threads, wood and papers etc. They discover the feel of grass and bark, fur and feathers and other natural phenomena, and will often savour the experience by holding objects against their cheeks or sucking them. Young children learn constantly through eyes and fingers, building up experience of the nature of things – their pattern, colour, form, texture and other characteristics which appear to be important to them.

The psychologist, Anton Ehrenzweig, in his book *The Hidden Order of Art*, states that the young child's vision is global, taking in the entire whole without differentiating it into its component details. He believes that the unconscious creative scanning which is taking place is far superior to discursive reason and logic. Ehrenzweig points out that at about eight years of age (at least, in Western civilisation) 'a dramatic change sets in in children's art. While the infant experiments boldly with form and colour in representing all sorts of objects, the older child begins to analyse these shapes by matching them against the art of the adult . . . and he usually finds his work deficient'. This finding is supported by many teachers and art educationalists, at least in the fact that a change is apparent, and that problems may well occur. (Franz Cizek noted this at seven years, and Rhoda Kellogg at eight years.)

Desmond Morris in *The Biology of Art* suggests that in the infant stages, art is a self-rewarding activity and experience in which, given the appropriate environment and circumstances, all children will involve themselves.

This phenomena and the fact that over the last century educationalists have become aware of an apparent broad universal pattern of development in the imagery of young children, has had a great bearing on education, but has led to some misunderstanding as to appropriate teaching methods. Teachers show respect and wonder at the delightful gradual unfolding of natural ability in the child and at the same time display a healthy fear of inhibiting the flow of creativity. But at times this can make them abdicate any semblance of structure, challenge, or real teaching. (Clearly we must later consider what is meant by the term 'teaching' in this context.)

The whole notion of 'Child Art', so crucial in its day in pointing out the intrinsic value of the child's work and the importance of lively experiences which led to the generation of artefacts, has quite rightly had a bearing on education in our schools. It allowed time, space, money and credence in educational terms to enable spontaneous expression. The work spoke for itself – but what of the child?

The misunderstanding apparent in some of our schools today is the belief that art always generates itself, that provided the child is given the tools, the time and the space, and the teacher 'encourages' and finally 'displays' the work, all will be well and art education has taken place. On this basis it would have seemed enough to appoint any member of staff who was interested and had 'flair' to be responsible for the art experience and curriculum in school. The fact that some very good work is often apparent in such cases does not change the argument that a deep knowledge and understanding of the child's development and needs is a necessity. The informed expectation of the teacher is of paramount importance, together with the ability to offer challenges and experiences at the appropriate time with an understanding of developmental sequence. The real and valuable contribution of the enthusiastic teacher which will shine through in any circumstance is, no doubt, the very quality of enthusiasm, together with the child's knowledge that their work is enjoyable and valued. When such teachers gain understanding and experience of the nature of art and of the child's development, they are second to none.

Much discussion has taken place regarding the nature of children's art in relation to adult fine art. For us, the most useful way, perhaps, would be to bypass the arguments if we can accept the fact that children and adults take part in artistic activity. E H Gombrich says 'There is no such thing as 'art' – there are only artists'. However, it is interesting to note certain apparent common denominators. First, artistic activity has undeniably been an important facet of human behaviour and is apparent from early history, continuing in unbroken sequence to the present day. It manifests itself in the lives of all races, irrespective of creed and culture, and has continued through war, peace and natural disasters. It is clearly a part, too, of our children's early life experience. We know from experience how freely in their early years they will scribble and enjoy materials, make images and decorate, often even before they can speak.

Second, man has used symbols and imagery to convey his ideas, his hopes and fears, relationships and responses to the world within him and without. He has used them in his rituals and magic, in his search for, or teachings about, his gods. He has believed that the image itself was or could become something greater than itself. He has used symbols and images to commemorate and record, for propaganda and advertisement and has used pattern to decorate and enhance himself, his belongings, his home and environment. He has used art forms in response to experiences and happenings in his life and in order to express his feelings and emotions.

What of our children? Is it not apparent that their art pertains to their lives and feelings? Their personal symbolism is based on the very stuff of living – their hopes, imaginings and fears, – themselves portrayed in many ways, friends and enemies, family, pets, possessions, homes and gardens. Beautiful things are celebrated, wars and horrors are played out, reality, imagination and fantasy interrelate. Colours, shapes and patterns are enjoyed for their own intrinsic qualities.

The certainty regarding the nature of fine art and children's art, is that it has little to do with simple imitation. It is always a by-product of thinking and feeling and not a mindless making of likenesses (although at its worst, some so-called art teaching comes near to this definition). William Blake said 'We are led to believe a lie when we see with and not through the eye'. The philosopher Susanne Langer regarded the nature of art 'as a non-discursive form of knowledge which is difficult to communicate in the form of language or indeed in any other form. It relies on our logical intuition of form perception'. We believe that this definition is as apt for the child as it is for the adult artist.

Chapter 1　Expectation

ONE OF THE MOST frightening aspects of our knowledge about educational performance is the realisation that by our own expectations, whether voiced or silent, we invite certain kinds of behavioural response. Taking into account the fact that the child's attitude and practice is also governed by personal expectations, it could well be argued that an understanding of this whole subject is crucial if we are to provide children with a sound education. It is therefore very important to consider three questions in regard to expectation from both the teacher and the child's viewpoint.

1　What do we think art really is?
2　What do we think is acceptable when we look at children's art?
3　What do we understand about the nature of seeing and personal perception?

What do we think art really is?

Teachers experienced in art and education will understand that there are many modes of expressing and communicating through visual and tactile forms. As we pointed out in the previous chapter, art is never mere imitation; any art form is one of many possible statements about some kind of human experience. There is nothing new in this and we can choose from any number of examples: cave paintings, early Egyptian art, Greek terracottas, Italian High Renaissance art, seventeenth century Dutch genre painting, French Impressionists, Expressionists, Surrealists, African sculpture, abstract painting, naive and folk art . . . Art forms make valid statements, but in very different 'languages'.

All of these ways of working offer us different aspects of reality in the way in which they transmit human thinking, working through materials. The invention of the camera offered a new and different kind of vision. The photograph was basically the production of a mechanism which would record (originally in monochrome) a section of the environment at which it was pointed, although the selection of the view, its definition and focus, was dependent on a human mind. The excitement caused by the selection of a random rectangle of nature was profound, following centuries of rule-based composition. The build-up over the years of more sophisticated photography, colour, moving pictures, film and video, has led some adults and children to the erroneous conclusion that the photographic image is the only real statement, and that the final aim of art is to be as close to it as is humanly possible. Photography has many valid functions and we are surrounded by its imagery, but the photograph is not a painting. The painting has a quality that a photograph can never have and cannot even imitate – the 'dynamic', or 'life force' in its own right, of the paint. It is also a product of a human mind, and can be used as a vehicle to distort, focus, analyse or express, at will. Clearly, the same can be said for drawings, sculpture, textiles or any other art forms.

As teachers, we should first question our own assumptions about the nature of imagery acceptable to us, and be willing to broaden our vision to include a rich variety of possibilities ranging through symbolism, analysis, abstraction, expression and experiment, both in the works of fine art we come across and in the art of children. By the age of seven or eight, our children may well have built up structures of what they consider to be acceptable practice in art and making judgements when looking at pictures, yet they have seldom, if ever, been overtly taught, and their vision is often very narrow. If we say that it is a 'natural development' and that all children demand a photographic realism, the argument does not stand up in the light of consideration of equally intelligent children in other parts of the world, and in other cultures, who do not have the same expectations.

Some art educationalists in the past have maintained that children's vision is pure and unsullied, and on no account should they be surrounded by images other than their own. Franz Cizek and his followers held this belief very strongly and many teachers will have encountered these views in their own training period.

We would maintain, however, that from his earliest years the child is building up material on which he is exercising his own critical faculty and expectation of what is acceptable *from whatever is around him in his environment*. In many cases this will be from home environment, television, magazines and newspapers, packaging, advertisement and comics. Twentieth century children already have an expectation of the nature of art and imagery before they come to school.

Can we afford to let their development stem from this narrow experience of art forms when we have the rich heritage of the arts worldwide and through the ages to offer?

Looking at children's art – a general pattern of sequential development

There are a number of theories of development of children's imagery with a surprising consensus of opinion in regard to the development and changes which actually take place. Differences only arise when there is consideration of interpretation, implications for the educator and strategy for teaching. We believe that the key to offering an appropriate art education lies in our ability to understand the development of children's imagery.

The dangers of defining any generalised sequence lie in oversimplifying what is really happening and neglecting to ask whether the structure is appropriate for every child. Nevertheless, providing it is considered as a pattern to which there may well be a variety of exceptions, such a sequence is a most useful tool to assist our understanding.

We believe that children work in five modes, moving from one to another as appropriate for the task in hand, or at will. (The ages quotes are added for general guidance only.)

1 **Experimentation and experience of materials and tools** (← 18 months – 18 years →)
2 **Symbolic interpretation** In the early years (← 3-7/8 years →) this will be based on wholistic scanning and global vision. It can continue into adult years as a valid option for communication and expression.
3 **Predominantly symbolist approach** At this stage (← 5-12 years →) the child will be showing a growing interest in a variety of items and a complexity of images; there will be evidence of a visual analytic approach in parts of the work.
4 **Predominantly analytic approach** (← 7/8 years → onwards) In this mode, the need for visual realism is paramount. Matching and comparisons are important, but symbolist overtones will often be apparent.
5 **Analytic approach** (← 8/9 years → onwards) This mode is characterised by visual realism based on personal experience through the senses and interpreted through the use of a variety of media.

Regarding the theories of development of children's imagery, we have a considerable body of expertise to call upon – Cizek, Burt, Lowenfeld and Brittain, Kellogg, Goodnow, Arnheim and Eisner to name but a few. Although the implications and interpretations can be very different, and at times contradictory, there is nevertheless a general consensus of agreement as to the developmental pattern.

SCRIBBLE

From babyhood the child will explore his world. No doubt some of his earliest experiences will be in kicking and moving his limbs, in touching and grasping. As he gains muscular control, his movements grow stronger and more varied, he can reach, and hold, and will begin to experiment and play with the items in his environment. The texture and feel of soft food on his plate, water and soap, mud and sand will offer him differing sensory experiences.

An early development is that of using tools to make effects. At first, this is probably an accidental, rather than a purposeful, happening – the manipulations of a spoon, chalk, pencil or felt tip pen causing marks – perhaps to his surprise. The enjoyment of this experience often lies in movement and its value is in the kinaesthetic and tactile realms.

A significant stage arises when the child realises he has made a mark, and from that point on the experience of movement is tempered with the enjoyment of seeing the marks made. This, in turn, appears to move on to an awareness of the nature of the marks, which, though at first random, are later repeated again and again. Whether the child uses a graphic tool, a brush, or responds to some malleable material will depend very much on what is available to him. Given clay or some other plastic material, he will parallel his 'scribble' experience by pushing his fingers into it, thumping, squeezing, prodding, pulling, flattening and rolling. As his manual ability develops we see divergence in ways of playing together with growing control.

Rhoda Kellogg, following research into children's drawing, isolated scribble into 20 basic types, consisting of a series of vertical, horizontal, diagonal, circular, curving, waving or zig zag lines and dots. These *basic scribbles*, she believes, are the building blocks out of which all art, pictorial and non-pictorial, is made. There are well-validated theories, too, for scribble forming a sound basis for the development of writing. There are also suggestions that in its analysis, readiness for shape recognition and reading are apparent and thus it is possible to identify the appropriate time for writing skills to be introduced (Rhoda Kellogg and Jacqueline Goodnow). The self-rewarding character of the activity is apparent in that the children, of their own initiative, will happily engross themselves again and again with drawing media, paint, clay, sand or any other available material.

The educational value surely must be seen in understanding the potential and control of materials and tools as well as in the initiation of ideas. Children deprived of this experience often need to be encouraged to 'play' with materials at a very much later stage, even in the secondary school, in order to build up confidence, and learn the value of experiment and control as well as the sheer enjoyment of expressive mark making and pattern.

ACCIDENTAL SHAPES

The child builds up a vocabulary of scribble movements and forms, and in so doing uses them in such a way that accidental shapes – crosses, squares, circles and triangles, as well as many amorphous forms – are apparent. These, too, will grow more complicated as energy and control build up and shapes are overlaid. A significant stage is reached when the child recognises a shape within the scribble, pointing to it, giving it some kind of name, or repeating the shape, often over and over again.

The circle or oval is very often the first shape to be recognised within the scribble. Possible reasons for this are diverse. Some psychologists suggest that the root lies in the child's early ability to distinguish and respond to the human face. Jung suggested that the circle is encoded in the human nervous system, and we have only to think of its significance in the life of our planet, with the sun and moon, pebbles, eggs, seeds, to name but a few examples.

Experience with paint will normally move through a soggy period of overlaid 'soup and custard' to a stage where areas and patches of colour are left without further overlays or obliteration. This activity will continue to widen the child's experience of materials and media and his own awareness of emerging shapes,

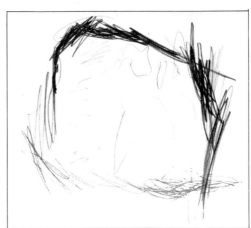
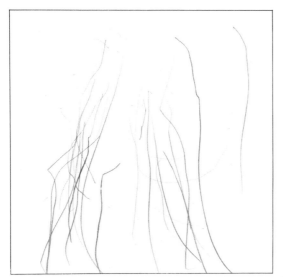

Scribble drawings. 2–4 years (showing development into early shape recognition and the beginning of the use of symbols).

'Mum and Cindy'. Girl 4 years.

together with the pleasures of colour and growing organisational powers. Three dimensional work will show greater ability to control, and often hand-sized pieces of clay or dough are shaped and squeezed into varying forms.

From this powerful basis of materials, pattern, colour, shape, form, and growing awareness, the child moves into an experience which is fundamental to the human being for the rest of his life. This is the ability to see analogies – to be reminded of one thing by touching or seeing another. Howard Gardner speaks of the child's growing self-knowledge, and the stage at which he links the world of graphic activity to the universe.

Note the personal involvement apparent in the subject matter.

'Me'. Girl 4 years.

Girl. 4 years. Yellow powder colour. 485 × 305 mms.

'Shouting'. Girl 4 years.

'It is snowing on the police car'. Boy 4 years.

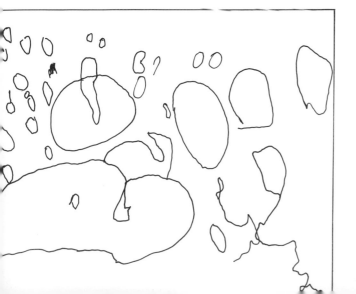

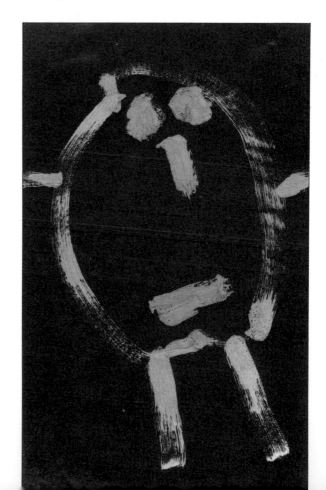

Very often this is apparent when children look at their scribble and 'recognise' a shape within it, *Look, I have painted a boat*, *These are railway lines*, or *It's an elephant*, being a few of many possible examples. When this stage is reached, although there will still be healthy sorties into 'scribble' and pattern, especially when new materials are introduced, much of the work will be based on premeditated content. Drawings, paintings and models are made in profusion. In two-dimensional work, overlapping seems to be taboo and children will go to great lengths to avoid breaking this self-imposed 'rule'. This is not surprising when we realise that the child is moving towards a symbolic mode of communication.

SYMBOLISM

The child is now moving into a mode of ordering his world, communicating and expressing his ideas through the use of personal symbols. (It is interesting to note how many of these symbols are common to children from different ethnic and cultural backgrounds). He may still enjoy a 'good scribble' at times, and will, given the opportunity, involve himself in bold painting with strong colours, as well as enjoying using graphic tools of all kinds, modelling in clay or other substances, building and constructing.

Rose Alschuler and Laberta Hattwick suggest that children's graphic work may pertain to communication, whilst painting is an emotive and expressive experience. Howard Gardner notes two 'types of approach', and labels children *patterners* and *dramatists*, although freely admitting that many children oscillate between the two modes – and others do not fit into them at all. Patterners, he suggests, arrange and re-arrange shapes and symbols, build with blocks and bricks, and are fascinated by order. Numbers and mathematics are often an interest. The children show no interest in naming their art products and are not socially inclined, although well able to understand and use speech. Dramatists play out their interests in 'pretend' and story telling. Conversation is the spice of life and they are interested in people and events. Their art mirrors these interests, and most products are named and often talked about at length. Once symbols emerge, considerable development is often apparent very quickly, with a proliferation of repeated symbols and new ones initially created over a matter of days, then gradually building up as time elapses.

The human figure is often the first to appear, being depicted in tadpole-like form with a large circle or oval with linear 'legs' and sometimes 'arms' attached. There are a number of theories regarding this image. Psychologists point out that interest in the human face, with its deep significance for the child, overrides all else. It is not difficult to understand that a symbolist will select characteristics and items he is most deeply interested in at that moment on that day and express his ideas in a hierarchy of scale, more often than not at their most recognisable angles. This should offer us a key to understanding children's work. Things, however, are not always what they seem; Jacqueline Goodnow and Rudolf Arnheim suggest that the large oval 'head' may well be a head/body image for some children. The challenge to add a 'belly button' will be 'answered' by many children by placing a firm dot, or 'o', under the mouth in the circular shape. It is clear too that children respond to rhythm and pattern; fingers on a hand, or legs on a donkey can be repeated again and again out of sheer enjoyment, although the child may well know the actual number.

The general discovery of the joys and possibilities of drawing, painting, and modelling things which are part of the child's life leads to a proliferation of figures, human and animal, houses, cars, trains, bicycles, trees, flowers and patterns. Colour often bears no relationship to reality and is freely enjoyed for its own sake. Hand and eye co-ordination improves and more control is apparent, together with a greater complexity of imagery, experience, knowledge and detail. The child will often fasten on to a mode of depicting a figure, house, tree, animal or any other object and repeat it again and again, adding embellishments as new experience demands. This basic mode is often known as a 'schema'.

Jacqueline Goodnow considers this stage to be apparent between 5 and 7 years, whilst Victor Lowenfeld believes that it develops between 7 and 9 years. In any case, what is going on in the child's experience is of significant educational value. He is using his art as a means to develop relationships and make concrete some of his

Infant group. Chalk and charcoal drawings in response to a challenge to draw themselves or their friends, following a movement session.
Note. *All children showed greater body and limb awareness.*

3–5 year old children dealing with the problem of bedtime. Note the differing ways of depicting themselves in relation to the bed.

Boy. 6 years. Felt tip. 160 × 250 mms.

'Lunchtime'. Girl. 6 years. Felt tip 145 × 195 mms.

Taking the dog for a walk. Boy. 5 years. Pencil. 140 × 215 mms.

Taking the dog for a walk. Boy. 5 years. Pencil. 230 × 245 mms.

thoughts. Jerome Bruner believes that imagery . . . 'characterises early intellectual functioning, being a precursor to later logical operations'. He sees each individual developing a knowledge of the world by seeking, choosing, organising and giving meaning to the environment through art. Daphne Plaskow suggests that drawing, painting and modelling 'crystalise visual impressions for the child, and put them into forms the mind can retain . . . Any kind of stimulation which encourages the child toward a greater understanding of the objects he sees around him, of his natural environment, and of aspects of his life in relation to others, will contribute to his intellectual maturation.' We would support the view that a very large part of a child's early education is built on and from art experience.

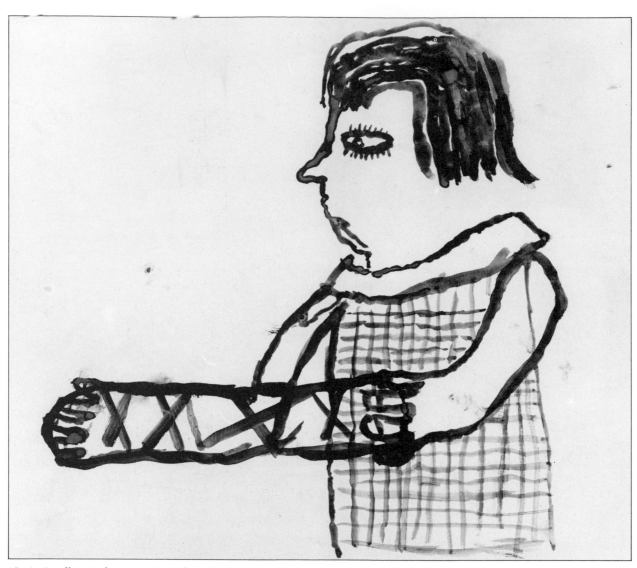

'Cat's Cradle'. Girl. 9 years. Powder colour and brush drawing. 300 × 310 mms.
Note *the full face eye in the profile head.*

'The Queen and her corgis walking in the palace grounds.' Girl. 9 years. Note the careful arrangement avoiding overlapping, and the components depicted from their most recognisable views (aerial view of lake – palace, trees, Queen and corgis' heads frontal view – corgis' bodies side view.)

Drawing of a friend. Boy. 8 years. Pencil. 500 × 375 mms.
Note 'analysis' of details in eyes, hands, teeth and pullover.
The placing of the classroom items and small boy behind the main figure is a new development.

Studies of the Headmaster. Junior group. Pencil.
Note *the variation in approach by these children from the same school.*

Lady with a Fan. (The teacher posing for children to draw, having stimulated them to see by a verbal introduction and discussion). Boy. 11 years. Charcoal. 370 × 300 mms.

Crouching Boy, (from life). Boy. 11 years. Pencil. 140 × 300 mms.

TOWARD THE ANALYTIC
STAGE

As the child matures and gains experience of his world, he becomes, it appears, aware of a need to use colour in such a way that in general terms it is representational. Grass will be green, sky is blue and flesh pink or brown. (This stage should not be confused with the ability to match.) His drawings often show a growing concentration on finely-observed detail and a mixture of visual and known characteristics will be apparent. At about the seventh or eighth year, the child (in Western civilisation) moves very strongly toward the need for his work to appear 'visually real' to him. He may grow disillusioned with his former imagery unless a sensitive teacher can show him that it is a *different* way of looking and working rather than an inferior one. The need for the young analyst to match and compare is strong in both two- and three-dimensional work. This is a stage where first-hand experience, investigation and wonder needs to be fostered, where visits to interesting environments should be planned, and where real objects to feel and look at for interest in colour, line, shape, texture, pattern and form should be introduced in great variety. To leave a child who is intellectually moving toward a need for the visually real, to soldier on with his waning interest in his personal symbolism, offering only titles and suggestions as stimuli, is disastrous. What many teachers consider to be a natural point for children to lose interest and become disillusioned with art, may be caused in reality by a lack of appropriate teaching.

As the child builds up experience and practice in the confident use of a variety of tools and materials, his response to his personal environment is more readily interpreted into line, shape, form, pattern and texture. The ability to interpret line, analyse shape, experience form, and match colour becomes apparent; proportion and depth are clearly problems to which he is beginning to apply his mind. There could be a danger at this stage in the introduction of mindless copying, mathematical perspective or generalised rules of proportion as these can deflect from the all-important challenge for real analysis in the form of first-hand investigation through looking, touching, and feeling.

The approaches to teaching for the two modes, the symbolic and the analytic, are totally different. Each will share the need for a rich input of first-hand experience and stimuli through visits, classroom displays, experience with objects, sounds, words, etc but whereas the young child, with a rich stimulating life in the classroom and elsewhere, and appropriate encouragement, will evolve his own art forms (suitable materials being provided) the older child will need sensitive challenge, guidance and appropriate teaching. Discussion regarding the child's expectation of the nature of art is crucial at this stage.

It is interesting to note that Victor Lowenfeld and W Lambert Brittain define the years between nine and eleven as the 'Gang age' and most teachers will be aware of group interaction becoming more predominant. Clearly we would do well to consider group work in a variety of approaches as part of children's education at this stage. The possibilities for enterprise, leadership, teamwork, working through difficulties, extending expectation of scale and depth, ideas, and uses of materials offer great potential in the hands of a sensitive teacher.

Note Howard Gardner quotes an experiment undertaken by Arthur B Clark in 1896 where children were challenged to make a drawing of an apple impaled by a pin. He noted that almost all of them were unable to make accurate depictions where the foreshortened pin entered one side of the apple, and emerged on the other side, until the middle years of the primary school (7–8 years).

Figure 1.1 shows some examples of the children's responses when this experiment was undertaken in a school in Suffolk.

It would be interesting to consider this kind of challenge alongside a collection of a child's work, in order to gain some insight as to the stage he has reached. It needs to be pointed out that the fact that a child is visually orientated rather than a symbolist or vice versa does not necessarily have any bearing on intellectual ability.

Figure 1.1

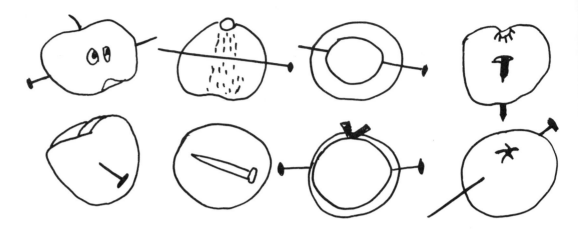

THE CHILD'S UNDERSTANDING OF ART

A six-year-old girl, on being given a set of felt-tipped pens for her birthday, drew a stiff little figure in a boat. The boat and the figure were made up of a variety of almost geometric shapes, each in a different colour; the face was blue and green and the hands were yellow. As she presented the drawing to the relative, who had given her the pens she asked, 'Does that look real?' The relative, a teacher, considered the question. If she answered yes, and the child had reached the analytic stage, the answer was clearly inappropriate. If no, and she was still entirely symbolist, this would not be acceptable either. In fact, she decided to return the question, 'What do you think?' she said. The answer was immediate. 'I know it's not real. I can draw real things when I want to but drawings don't always have to be real, do they?'

Why do we find answers of this kind so surprising? Do we actually talk to our children and listen to what they have to say about their work and what they believe to be true? This child was quite clearly able to sort out the fact that there was more than one way of making judgements about art *and at the age of six she could bring to bear different criteria for looking at drawings.*

'Instrumentalists'. Boy. 6 years. Pencil. 240 × 415 mms.
This drawing was made a few hours after a concert given by a group of musicians in the school.
This pupil has a strong visual memory, and spent much of his time at home drawing for pleasure. His special interests were in 'Star Wars' figures which he ably animated for his own imaginative purposes. Literally hundreds of drawings were made. His age and approach are a salutary reminder that there will always be some children who do not fit into accepted age band or developmental expectations.

Taking this into consideration, a number of teachers worked with children to gain further insight into their understanding of art and their basis for making judgements. With the children, they looked at the work of artists, together with ongoing work in the classroom, and put a number of questions, in a conversational way, to individuals or groups.

What kind of a picture/model, do you think this is?
What do you think the person who painted/drew/made this was trying to tell us?
Can you describe this picture/model?
Do you like, or dislike it? Why?

The children showed interest in all cases and conversed freely. Some had difficulty in finding words (these were not necessarily the very young ones), while others began quickly to extend their vocabulary. A consensus of terms often built up over a number of sessions and interest did not wane.

Pictures with subject matter became 'story pictures' and the children would happily describe what was going on. Analytical and descriptive pieces of work were described as 'matching pictures' or ones 'where you tried to make it look like things'. There were also 'colour pictures' and 'pattern pictures'. Models showed 'how people were feeling', or 'what they were like', or things with 'nice shapes'. An interesting development was with groups of 7–9 year olds, some of whom were at 'symbolic' stages of development, whilst others had moved to the analytic approach. These groups were found to be readily 'sorting' their peers' work into 'story pictures' or 'matching pictures'. The symbolist, who may well have seen his own work as less acceptable, and might possibly have been moving towards an 'I can't draw' approach, gained new confidence when his friends accurately described his 'story' or subject matter. Later the approach of the symbolist was consolidated when the teacher introduced reproductions of works by Chagall, Paul Klee, Fra Angelico and Sassetta.

Older children (8, 9, 10 and 11 year olds) read more into the artefacts, sometimes showing great insight and sensitivity and using interesting vocabularies. They responded to aesthetic qualities and commented on feelings, shapes, pattern and colour. Interest in the names of the artists, where and when they lived, and other insights into their lives and times became apparent.

Discrimination, and the realisation that there are different bases for judgemental decision making, are no mean achievement for children of this age, yet we found that these skills could be easily and naturally developed, the children deriving much pleasure and considerable insight from the practice.

Vision and touch: the nature of 'seeing', 'feeling' and personal perception

The third significant area in which expectation plays a part pertains to vision and touch, and the nature of seeing and feeling. 'We see what we expect to see' is nearer the truth, perhaps, than we imagine. Examples of the fallibility of eyewitness reports of happenings are often before us in the newspapers and on television. We cannot believe our eyes unless we really know how to see with them when it's necessary.

One experiment which might convince us that we are not, in fact, as observant as we might believe is given as an example of selective vision. A number of groups of teachers were asked, individually, to describe their own watch faces, without first looking at them. In no group were more than 7% found to be accurate and a large proportion of the remainder had often confidently given descriptions which were fundamentally inaccurate (for example, black faces instead of white and vice versa, or Roman numerals, when only spots were apparent!).

As teachers, we need to be able to 'see' when we attune ourselves to look, and we need, too, to be able to describe, in a visual and lively way, what we see. Seeing is a skill, pertaining to many parts of the curriculum in addition to the aesthetic and creative area – nature and environmental studies, science and mathematics to name but a few.

With children of 7–8 upwards it can be fascinating to consider analytical drawing (two- or three-dimensional) as a vehicle to enable seeing and understanding rather

than vice versa, and the resulting studies can be interesting pieces of evidence in considering the child's stage of development. Frederick Frank in *The Zen of Seeing*, writes

> 'It is in order to really see, to see ever deeper, ever more intensively, hence to be fully aware and fully alive that I draw what the Chinese call 'the ten thousand things' around me. Drawing is the discipline by which I constantly rediscover the world. I have learned that what I have not drawn, I have never really seen, and that when I start drawing an ordinary thing, I realise how extraordinary it is, a sheer miracle.'

The discipline of studying every part of an item or area intensely, as well as seeing it as a whole, is a necessity in this kind of work. It requires a skilful and lively use of words on the part of the teacher to engender this intense concentration. It is a sobering thought that poor response on the part of the pupil may well reflect the teacher's lack of skill rather than the child's.

There are, of course, many ways of analysing. It would be simplistic to consider that a true likeness of say, a tree, should aim to be 'photographic'. Very different drawings or models may result in response to challenges to study shape, pattern, movement, mood, how it grows, or the spaces in between the branches . . .

Children are no exception to the prejudices of vision we find within ourselves, and it is our responsibility as teachers to lead them to the skills of seeing and touching. We may have much to learn ourselves first, for until we become visually sensitive we cannot help the children to any depth of experience.

The interaction between words and visual experience is beautifully portrayed in *The Curtains* a poem by Steven Cave (aged 10). It is interesting to consider what kind of teaching must have gone on prior to the writing of this poem which is so strongly visual:

Open the curtains please,
get some light in this room.
Get rid of the darkness and have some light.

Let's look at the sun.
Let's look at the roses.
Let's look at the wet grass.
With a carpet of dew on it.

Look, just enjoy this moment. It won't,
It won't happen again, I know it won't.
Look, just look through the glass in the window.

See the sky, see other houses
Look at anything you can.
Just look.

Regarding tactile qualities, we are sometimes inclined to take for granted the sensory experience of touching and the amount of experience we gain through feeling. Information pertaining to form, shape, scale, temperature, weight, texture and quality are all conveyed to us through the sensitivity of our hands. The information interacts with vision. Kimon Nicolaides says 'Merely seeing is not enough. It is necessary to have a fresh vivid physical contact with the object you draw, through as many senses as possible, and especially through the sense of touch.'

Silhouettes. Studies from life. 9 years. Paint. 260 × 120 mms.

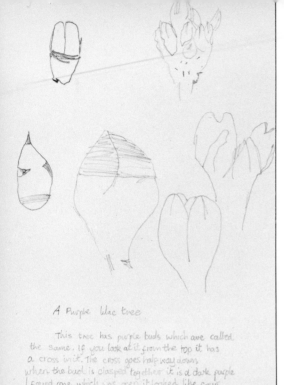

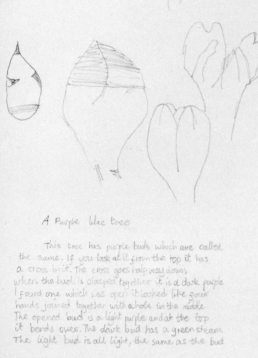

A Purple lilac tree

This tree has purple buds which are called the same. If you look at it from the top it has a cross in it. The cross goes half way down when the bud is clasped together it is a dark purple. I found one which was open it looked like four hands joined together with a hole in the middle. The opened bud is a light purple and at the top it bends over. The dark bud has a green steam. The light bud is all light, the same as the bud

Study of buds. Boy. 10 years. Pencil.
235 × 210 mms. Art, science or language?!

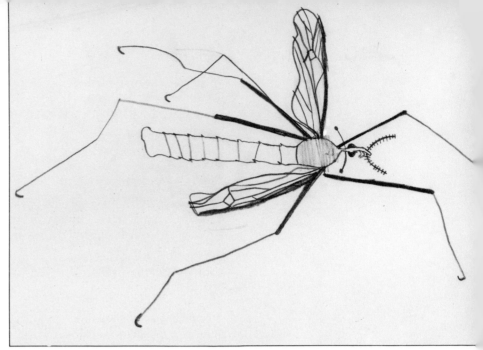

'Daddy-long-legs'. Girl. 10 years. Pencil. 220 × 300 mms.

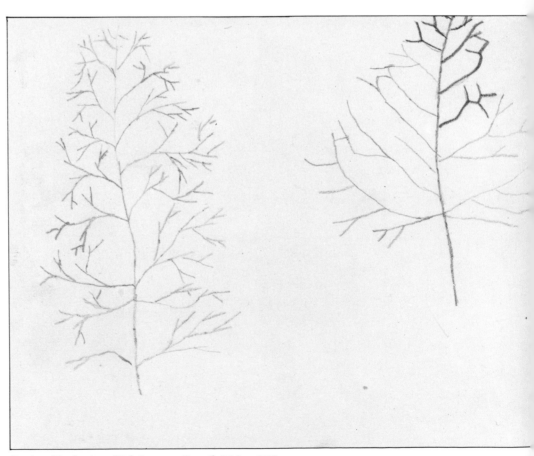

Study of leaf veins. Girl. 9 years. Pencil. 205 × 250 mms.
The children were asked to draw the veins of the leaf. Having done so one child said 'Look, I have drawn a lovely tree'.

Hornplayer. Boy. 11 years. Ink and Paint. 395 × 235 mms.

Chapter 2 The Power of Words
Stimulation and motivation for creative work

ONE OF THE KEYS to motivating children to respond with interest and vigour to the endless variety of experience life can offer is to involve them in a personal and emotive way. To create artefacts can be a cold, external experience in which the child will comply with the teacher's requests, having estimated the teacher's involvement and allocating the amount of effort he deems to be required for his response. If, on the other hand, the teacher can stimulate the child to 'live' the experience in imagination by the use of descriptive and evocative words, an internalised and personal response is apparent. We know that memories are dormant within us until triggered by reminders in the form of sensory experience or words and it is on this ground that the teacher can build with confidence. This approach can be a valuable component in the child's art education and non-specialist teachers have much to offer, providing they have the ability to immerse themselves in an experience and are able to communicate its vitality in words.

Yehudi Menuhin speaks of four fields of experience in his essay 'The Compleat Education'. These are:

1 Man versus infinity – embracing all that he can never understand
2 Man versus his physical environment as reported by his senses
3 Man versus other men and other life
4 Man versus himself

'Man's whole history' he states 'has been an effort to reconcile and integrate these fields'. This is mirrored in the world's art, past and present, and is embryonically apparent in children's work.

It is interesting to consider these four areas and to ask ourselves whether we extend our teaching in all or only some of the fields. Much of children's art pertains to sensitive response, learning, ordering and coming to terms with life, and embraces a deep involvement in experiences, remembered and imagined. How can we encourage these things to happen? It must surely be by relating sensitively to the subject matter and to the children, using a variety of resources, skilfully communicating and triggering memory or stimulating imagination so that they can live, or relive an experience. This will entail an immersion of the whole self in all aspects of our sensory awareness – sight, touch, hearing, smell and taste. At the beginning of a project the teacher will need to undertake what can be described as a 'lighting up time'! This introduction may take the form of first-hand visual stimuli, a poem, or prose, the teacher's description, discussion or conversation with the children. Although there can be no general rule regarding the length of time spent in this way, it would not be considered out of proportion to use up to one fifth of the working time in order to establish depth of involvement.

It is interesting to note that some question and answer sessions can dissipate expressive and communicative energy. A certain amount of damming up of ideas for later expression in a chosen media is worth experimenting with. This enables the child who is slow to develop his own ideas and to consider his own contribution without disturbing influences from those who respond immediately – and sometimes super-ficially. It is always possible for the teacher to deal encouragingly with those who wish to contribute by saying 'Don't tell me now, you can show me in your painting/model, etc.' One aspect of the skill of drawing out a memory experience is to pose a challenge followed by a series of questions – always making sure that an open-ended approach allows opportunity for the child to conjure a personal image not already mentioned. For example, following a discussion about cats, a teacher challenged the children to conjure up a mind picture of a cat they knew,

'Have you chosen one you love, or one you are afraid of? Do you enjoy looking at it, or playing with it? or does it make you sneeze? . . . Who does it belong to (think about it, don't answer . . .) is it your own? or one of your relative's? or a friend's? or perhaps someone you do not know . . . ? What colour is it? Is it black? or ginger? tabby? white? tortoiseshell? grey – or Siamese? or some other colour? . . . Does it have long fur, or short, what does it feel like when you touch or stroke it? Is it rough, or smooth? Imagine stroking it gently from the tip of its nose, over its head, down its back . . . what does it do when you stroke it? . . . What shape are its ears? are they pointed or round . . . ? how do they feel when you touch them gently?
. . . What kind of tail does it have? Is it fluffy, or bushy, or thin, – long or short? . . . What colour are its eyes? are they amber or green, yellow, blue, or some other colour . . . What shape are its eyes? . . . What shape are the dark pieces in the middle of its eyes? Have you ever noticed that they change shape when the light is bright, or when it is out in the dark? . . . What kind of whiskers does your cat have? . . . How do they grow? . . . What kind of nose? . . . Look at its paws . . . what are they like, can you see the claws, or not? . . . Is it a friendly cat? or is it fierce or spiteful? . . . Is it playful or lazy or has it got some other kind of character? Do you know its name? . . . Where is your cat and what is he or she doing? Is it indoors or outside? What kind of a day is it? Is it hot or cold, wet or dry? . . . Imagine that you are very close to it so that you can see it in every detail . . . See if you can show me what your cat is really like.'

This stimulus could lead to drawing, painting, modelling, collage, printmaking or writing. The description is aiming to introduce a number of trigger points which might inspire the child to build up his own picture, rather than have one imposed by the teacher. It is a worthwhile exercise whether or not it leads to creative work. There is a wealth of suitable visual language excerpts from stories, poems, songs, exciting descriptions in travel or nature books . . . It is useful for teachers to build up their own collections for use in a variety of contexts.

Successfully enabling a child to 'live' in his imagination can afford him many varied experiences. It can also have a marked effect on his interest in reading and writing as he begins to see the enriching possibilities of a personal involvement in and enjoyment of the subject matter.

AREAS OF EXPERIENCE AND EXAMPLES OF POSSIBLE STIMULI FOR CREATIVE WORK

The following are just some of the areas of experience which offer many possibilities for creative work:

- Children's personal response to *infinity* – life and death, dreams, legends, phantasy, mystery, from first-hand experience, stories, poems, music, etc.
- Children's personal response to their *environment* – the living world, nature, the elements, land, sea, air, fire and water, the world of plants, weather, buildings, machinery. Opportunities for children to offer from first hand experience, memory and imagination, the world they live in, or stimulated responses from stories, poems, etc.
- Children's personal responses to *people and other living things* – family; friends, animals, insects, birds, fish, situations, groups, individuals, characters, first-hand experience, memory, imagination or phantasy. A real involvement of personal response and feeling should be encouraged.
- Children's consideration of *their own responses* – personal feelings, emotions, relationships, responses in the context of everyday life, imagined situations, etc.

'Zaccheus'. Girl. 9 years. Coloured felt tips. 370 × 480 mms.

The elements of art – colour, line, pattern, texture, tone, shape, form, embrace all the foregoing areas as well as being unique to the discipline of art. Paintings, pattern, print, relief, models, sculpture, collage, and textiles afford children opportunities to enjoy, experiment, celebrate, create, analyse and record their sensory experiences.

VISUAL STIMULI

James Reeves' three-verse poem entitled *Fireworks* offers a lively stimulus for painting, collage, wax resist etc. The language is evocative of mood and atmosphere, as well as visual effects.

Fireworks

They rise like sudden fiery flowers
That burst upon the night,
Then fall to earth in burning showers
Of crimson, blue and white.

Like buds too wonderful to name,
Each miracle unfolds,
And catherine-wheels begin to flame
Like whirling marigolds.

Rockets and Roman candles make
An orchard of the sky,
Whence magic trees their petals shake
Upon each gazing eye.

Bonfire night is one of the occasions when excitement reaches it peak just before the event and can be built on the memory and enjoyment of past years together with anticipation of the coming celebration.

William Blake's famous line *Tyger, Tyger burning bright in the forests of the night* can be sufficient stimulus as it stands, providing the teacher is able to involve the children in projecting themselves into this breathtaking jungle in the darkness.

Another tiger poem which offers beautifully descriptive language is *India* by W J Turner.

India

They hunt, the velvet tigers of the jungle,
The spotted jungle full of shapeless patches –
Sometimes they're leaves, sometimes they're hanging flowers,
Sometimes they're hot gold patches of the sun:
They hunt, the velvet tigers of the jungle!

What do they hunt by glimmering pools of water,
By the round silver Moon, the pool of Heaven:
In the striped grass, amid the barkless trees –
The Stars scattered like eyes of beasts above them!

What do they hunt, their hot breath scorching insects,
Insects that blunder wildly in the way,
Vividly fluttering – they also are hunting,
Are glittering with a tiny ecstasy!

The grass is flaming and the trees are growing,
The very mud is gurgling in the pools,
Green toads are watching, crimson parrots flying,
Two pairs of eyes meet one another glowing –
They hunt, the velvet tigers in the jungle.

Children are always interested in changes in scale: Gulliver, Tom Thumb, Mrs Pepperpot, Alice in Wonderland all offer possible subject matter. Hugh Finn's poem *The Beetle* takes this concept further.

A Beetle caught my eye, one day,
  Beside the path;
There, with his head buried deep in a daisy-centre,
Pigging and bolting it – great, scented, yellow mouthfuls –
  With the space he had already eaten
  Blackened around him;
There he gorged, standing on his ridiculous, gluttonous head,
  With his hard, thin legs
  Straight up in the forgotten air,
And his head deep in a dim, succulent heaven.

This kind of poem could be interpreted freely or form a challenge to children to take a 'bird's eye view' of a world of a different scale. Analytical work with children searching flower heads and leaves, and studying insects through lenses and magnifying glasses, extends and enriches learning, communication and expression. *The Science 5–13* project 'Minibeasts' offers further development on this theme.

There are many 'colour' poems or prose excerpts which can enrich and extend colour experience. These, in conjunction with displays and personal collections can deepen a child's enjoyment and understanding of colour potential. Mary O'Neill's poem *What is White?* offers a less usual but rich vocabulary on the subject, with a variety of suggestions:

White is a dove
And lily of the valley
And a puddle of milk
Spilled in an alley –
A ship's sail,
A kite's tail,
A wedding veil,
Hailstones and
Halibut bones
And some people's
Telephones.
The hottest and most blinding light
Is white.
And breath is white
When you blow it out on a frosty night.
White is the shining absence of all colour
Then absence is white
Out of touch
Out of sight
White is marshmallow
And vanilla ice-cream
And the part you can't remember
In a dream.
White is the sound
Of a light foot walking
White is a pair of
Whispers talking.
White is the beautiful
Broken lace
Of snowflakes falling
On your face.
You can smell white
In a country room
Near the end of May
When the cherries bloom.

Many stories offer powerful visual stimuli and most teachers will compile their own personal anthologies of suitable material, which they can bring to life. One particularly good example is Oscar Wilde's *Selfish Giant*. This is how Wilde describes the Giant's final sight of his winter garden, showing signs of spring:

'It was certainly a marvellous sight. In the farthest corner of the garden was a tree quite covered with lovely white blossoms. Its branches were golden, and silver fruit hung down from them, and underneath it stood the little boy he had loved.'

The theme of dragons is always a popular one. J R R Tolkien's *The Hobbit*, the *Beowulf* story and *St George and the Dragon* fables provide exciting narratives.

For the young child, the teacher's narration of a highly visual story or poem can end with the suggestion that it would be lovely to make a painting, drawing or model. The child may or may not follow up the suggestion, but the possibility has been introduced, and they may well begin to visualise. The stimuli may prove equally relevant to language, creative writing, drama, dance, music and song.

An example of word stimuli. 'Man with his arms full of stars.'

The teacher gave a group of ten children the stimulus '*A man with his arms full of stars*'. He asked the children to reflect quietly on this image for a moment and then offered them paper and pencil for writing, and printing rollers, poster paints, printing inks, scrap card and large pieces of variously coloured sugar paper, for art. The children divided into two groups. He encouraged them to use as wide a variety as possible of the materials, and gave them two hours, to complete, he hoped, both tasks. They were promised that, if necessary, more time could be found on the following day.

The children were 'taken' with the image (which had come to the teacher during the night!) and all produced excellent work. The printing/painting used all the given art materials in various ways, as well as several techniques, including scrap material printing, finger painting, and roller printing (see page 61). It was of exceptional quality, as was the poem, which was runner up in the W H Smith Young Writer's Competition for 1982.

I saw a man

I saw a man with his arms full of stars
He was puzzled about humans and their ways
He was in a hurry and was hot tempered
He didn't see me creeping through the darkness.

The stars tickled his eyes as he wandered
He gazed into space, still gripping tightly the stars
They were like crystals floating through his hands
And then gone for ever.

If I had the chance to touch those crystals
Which skim and slip and move,
I definitely would touch them
Before the shadows fall.

[Rachel Wardley's poem was published in 'Young Writers 1982' published by Heinemann.]

The prerequisite for the work was as follows: the children had been sensitised to various materials; they had been encouraged to make choices – of materials especially; and they had been read literally hundreds of poems, and shown many different kinds of pictures. They had been taught over a long period of time implicitly, if only rarely explicitly that their verbal and pictorial images could be of high value. This slow painstaking build-up was of more importance than the immediate stimulus.

'Cats'. The power of words – visuality, drawing and writing. 10–11 years. White and black chalk on sugar paper.

Cat

The cat stalks through the grass
searching for food, his eyes glow in the
dark like two torches in the night,
his legs move jaggedly ready to pounce.
The black conker sniffs a mouse,
the cat's movement get faster and faster
till it turns into a sprint,
the mouse ducks into his hole,
the cat gives up and slows down,
he walks back purring like a baby crying

The big green marbles.
Stuck in The middle
of a mass of fur.
he Stalks like a ghurka
running, jumping and bouncing
like it's got Springs on
on The bottom of it's paws.
It pounces
like a glider taking off

250 × 295 mms.
Boy. 8 years.

'In a forest' (following a word stimulus encouraging the children to think how they would feel
in this situation).
11 years. Pen and ink drawings on sugar paper. 280 × 290 mms.

Chapter 3 Art Education
The Role of the Headteacher and Staff

*T*HE WHOLE area of Creative and Aesthetic experience will need careful consideration and should include a strong element of art, craft, visual communication and display. We believe that it is important that a structure which is flexible enough to allow and incorporate a variety of enthusiasms and responses should be set up in schools. The curriculum should offer the child the privilege of a broad developmental experience in two- and three-dimensional art together with an understanding of the nature of the discipline. Children should be given opportunity to enjoy, discuss and critically respond to a variety of art, craft and design forms.

Gone are the days when art experience could be seen as a timefiller, given to children when the 'real work' was finished – the meaningless challenge, teacher-directed end-product, or copy.

In looking at art and craft in the curriculum, in 1978, the Department of Education and Science published a book entitled *Art in Junior Education*. In its conclusion it offers nine discussion points which are obviously aimed at Head-teachers. We believe them to be relevant in this context, and are therefore quoting them in full.

1 Is there an effective policy for ensuring consistency of good environmental standards throughout the school? Are there sources of informative and inspirational material of quality for all reasonable purposes? Are these used?

2 Is there a policy for development and progress for each child according to his capabilities? Are there plans for the development of content and skills in the use and understanding of colour, shape, texture, pattern, form? Is there a programme for the development of appreciation of pictures, objects and buildings?

3 Have pupils and teachers high expectations and standards of achievement in visual knowledge, memory and interpretation?

4 Is there adequate time to learn to observe; in the classroom or in local or more distant environments; through interest and compulsion arising from many areas of the curriculum in which an awareness of form, order, pattern, design and colour is essential, and for which training and practice are necessary?

5 Is there an awareness of the special relationship with language development? with science and mathematics? with humanities and environmental studies?

6 Does any teacher act as a consultant in art? How does he/she operate? If there is no consultant, might the work benefit if a member of staff were so appointed?

7 How are skills taught? What progress is expected? How are stages recorded and assessed?

8 How are materials, tools, chosen, ordered, organised, maintained?

9 What in-service activities are required to promote further skill and understanding? Are there suitable sources of teachers' reference materials within reach? Do the teachers know them? Do they use them?'

However small the school, it will be necessary for the Head or a designated teacher with appropriate understanding and background to be responsible for this area of experience. This may mean that an existing member of staff needs to be encouraged to seek advice, undertake inservice courses, visits, reading and practical work. Trained art specialists are only appropriate if they also have expertise in primary teaching, and their role in first schools – with a few exceptions – will be that of classteacher. Some flexibility of timetabling, or team teaching, should allow for a sharing of strengths.

In larger schools designated posts should be considered and the role clearly defined by the Headteacher. Depending on school structure, size and management, different groupings may be considered: Visual Arts, Art and Design, Expressive Arts or Creative and Aesthetic areas of the curriculum, for example. Environment, visual communication and display is sometimes considered as a part of this responsibility, or in its own right.

The role of the teacher responsible for Art will include the following:
- responsibility for the formulation of policy regarding the visual arts in the school;
- acting as consultant, adviser and in-service organiser for other members of staff;
- responsibility to keep up-to-date through attending inservice courses, making visits and reporting back to the staff;
- class teaching;
- responsibility for advising on and ordering tools, equipment and materials;
- responsibility for initiating liaison with schools to which pupils will proceed and with other pyramid schools;
- responsibility for visual imagery and experience through the use of original works, artists, craftsmen, loan schemes, books and other media.

Visual communication and display may be seen as part of the role, or separated from it provided appropriate liaison and teamwork is envisaged.

The Headteacher will need to convince every member of staff of the importance of balance in education and the need to undertake basic in-service experience especially in areas where they feel they have little understanding or flair. Clearly, the Education Authority must play a part in offering appropriate courses. Active encouragement for members of staff to attend these to extend their experience and to set up in-school in-service experience will be a necessary ingredient for development.

Open discussion at staff meeting level will no doubt bring out a number of hopes, fears and questions.

Sheila Paine writes in *Six Children Draw*

'Teachers and others involved in education and working with children and adolescents, have given a deal of attention to early drawings, allowing (and assuming) them to flow naturally and meaningfully in infancy and pre-adolescence and attempting to develop and extend the facility through the secondary stage of schooling. But belief about art and drawing in educational practice presents a series of dramatic conflicts (is it play or work? is it a 'gift' or something to be mastered? can it be learned but not taught? is it meaningful or irrelevant to life? is it without 'rules' or can it be controlled and assessed by them?) which bedevil art teachers and their pupils.'

This passage highlights some of the dilemmas teachers face, together with many different approaches and expectations from individuals, depending on when and where they originally trained. Added to this there are many who feel that they were, or are, no good at art and would prefer to abdicate the responsibility to more gifted colleagues. This is often a mistake, on two scores. First, it is not possible to separate the actual process of making and doing from the thinking that goes on in the classroom. Second, it is possible for an open-minded primary teacher to offer a sound art education by gaining experience through an understanding of art and the children's development within it. The fears of some teachers that they lack 'drawing ability' and will be 'found wanting' are groundless, in the early years. Experienced art teachers seldom, if ever, draw for children in the context of art experience; the children would invariably copy the teacher's drawing rather than come to terms with their own seeing, understanding and imagery. Skill and real expertise is involved in art education and will be dealt with in a later chapter, but first and foremost comes the crucial matter of expectation.

We believe what really happens in art education depends far more on the teacher's understanding of the nature of art, children's development and the ability to see and communicate the marvellous potential of the natural and man-made world, than on the teacher's own artistic abilities.

Teacher skills and role

Teachers must critically appraise their own perceptions and expectations regarding art, and be honest with themselves as to whether they really understand the development of the child's imagery. It is important, too, that they recognise the underlying educational value of the experiences involved. If they concentrate on a series of teacher-directed end products, rather than on the value and learning processes within the work, the real worth can be lost.

In one case a teacher challenged a group of nine- and ten-year-old children to make an intensive study of a stuffed owl. After the session the owl was returned to the museum. A number of children made studies of parts of the bird, rather than the whole, but the teacher, in selecting work to put on display, chose only those pieces which were, in her eyes, 'finished'. More appropriate criteria for judging the work would have been the quality of involvement, real 'seeing' and response to the stimulus. In this instance, the 'finished' piece of work had no more relevance than it would have in a page of sketches and studies by Leonardo da Vinci, Henry Moore, or any other artist or student, searching and ordering experience through drawing. The whole process should be seen as a means to a much broader end, entailing personal involvement, 'seeing', skills of tool and media handling, communication, expression and problem solving.

Although on many occasions children will naturally think in terms of a single piece of work, they should be encouraged to follow it up, where time allows, with a second piece – or a series. This process, together with challenges to undertake a number of pieces of experimental work (which often leads to a climax) will change the children's expectation, and often reveals very interesting sequences of development which might not have been apparent in other circumstances. It is an interesting anomaly that often only when we move our concentration away from 'end products' do the most valuable pieces of work occur.

Much has been said regarding the teacher's role. Theories range from laissez faire attitudes, which aim to encourage a so-called freedom of expression, to heavily directed teaching, based on rigid systems and techniques. Our recommendations stress the need for an overall development structure within which, with sensitive teaching support and challenge, the child is able to find his own way and develop in an individual manner. The skills required for this positive approach are embodied in all that is best in the teacher's classroom attitude – enthusiasm and interest, lively communication and imaginative use of resources. It is necessary for the teacher to have an understanding of imagery, and also practical experience of the tools and materials which the child is expected to use.

We recommend that teachers of children in the 7–11 age-range gain experience of looking and recording through drawing (in a variety of media) at their own level. The importance lies in understanding the process concerned, rather than in the end product. Teachers who find their own work unsatisfactory can, nevertheless, challenge and stimulate children to go well beyond their own capabilities.

There are six key areas relating to the teacher's role:

1 THE POTENTIAL OF THE CLASSROOM ENVIRONMENT

The classroom environment should facilitate the many activities necessary for the child's education. The teacher should consider:
- organisation of areas for practical work – wall, floor, table tops, easels etc;
- organisation of tools, equipment and materials;
- organisation for the use of water;
- arrangement and use of display areas.

It is useful to review, at frequent intervals, whether we are making the best use of our facilities, and to experiment with alternative arrangements.

QUESTIONS

Are children organised in such a way as to enable practical and other activities to take place without interference?
Are practical areas well situated in relation to entries and exits, water sources etc?
Is the workshop layout of tools, materials and equipment appropriately organised in relation to work areas, congested areas etc?
Do the children know and understand the organisation, and places for storage of tools and equipment?
Do the children understand the need for care in handling tools, equipment and materials?
Are tools and materials of appropriate quality to enable good work?
Is work displayed in such a way that children can experience and learn from it?

2 THE POTENTIAL OF TOOLS, EQUIPMENT AND MATERIALS

Since communication and expression in art occur by means of materials and tools, it is important that the teacher has practical experience of them. The message embodied in any art form is part and parcel of the 'life force' or 'dynamic' generated by the media. A drawing has a different quality from a print, and textiles, clay and paint have characteristics of their own. Too often, it seems, teachers are aware only of the 'subject matter' presented, not realising that this subject matter is diminished if they do not consider materials and means.

QUESTIONS

Are tools and materials of appropriate quality to enable good work?
Are pencils appropriately sharp?
Do scissors cut?
Is clay of the right consistency?
Are adhesives appropriate for the tasks?
Are rich colours available?

It is interesting to note that if teachers do try out the tools and materials on offer, some major changes can take place!

3 THE TIME FACTOR IN RELATION TO CREATIVE WORK

In most cases, teachers at this stage of schooling will be responsible for the organisation of the whole curriculum and time allocation for the school day. Any art activities, to have real value, require careful consideration and a flexible approach dictated by the nature of the work in hand. Some children work methodically and with great care, and require long stretches of time to complete their work. Others work very swiftly and may, if given the opportunity, carry out more than one piece of work in a stretch.

Whatever the case, it is important that children feel secure in the knowledge that they can immerse themselves in their work, in an unhurried way. Some challenges may use the constraints of time in order to generate a sense of urgency (for example, experimental games or quick drawings of moving things) but in the main the security of having appropriate time for the task is important. (It is, of course, understood that balance between areas of the curriculum will be restored at other times in the working week.)

QUESTIONS

Has the teacher considered the time scale necessary for working with various materials for specific challenges?
Has the teacher considered a flexible approach, allowing children an appropriate stretch of time for the full development of a piece of work or a sequence of pieces?

4 THE POTENTIAL OF FIRST-HAND RESOURCES FOR STIMULATING WORK

A variety of resources, including natural and manmade objects and artefacts, should play their part as everyday necessities in children's education. Nothing can take the place of first-hand study and experience, both in and outside school. The steady build-up of knowledge and understanding about the nature and qualities of things cannot be gained in any other way, and this forms a sound basis for all aspects of learning.

QUESTIONS
Do children have sufficient opportunities to go out into the environment and to enjoy it, respond to it and learn from it in a positive way?
Are there at all times interesting displays of natural and/or manmade objects in the classroom? Are the children encouraged to be aware of them and respond to them?
Are magnifying glasses and lenses available for children to use in studying displays?
Are original works of art, craft and design brought into school for children to discuss?
Has the teacher considered inviting artists and craftsmen into school?
Does a collection of reproductions of art form part of the basic classroom resources equipment?
Does the book corner/library contain books with reproductions of art and design forms of all kinds (including buildings) past and present?
Do the children's reading books contain a variety of good quality illustrations?
Does the teacher make use of loan schemes to obtain present day and historic images for the children to discuss and enjoy?

5 THE POWER OF WORDS TO HEIGHTEN EXPERIENCE AND EVOKE IMAGES

Enthusiasm is the key which will open many doors, educationally. Many adults, thinking back to their own schooldays, can remember the life and interest generated in a subject by a lively teacher. What part did the use of words play in communicating this enthusiasm? Some of the most successful teachers are those whose use of language is imaginative and evocative.

We all respond to visual triggers, and could, no doubt, list many. 'Like a cobweb' . . . 'like a crackling, blazing fire' . . . 'like tree branches against the sky' . . . 'like a sweetshop counter' . . . such phrases may conjure up memories and meaning. Words describing sounds and scents also help to remind us of experiences deep within our memory.

Teachers who feel they lack experience in some aspects of art education can often gain confidence by working with language based on experience (see *The power of words* p 24).

QUESTIONS
Does the teacher use evocative and descriptive language to stimulate children's imagination and memory?
Are children encouraged to use words descriptively with regard to visual and tactile stimuli?
Does the classroom/school library include sufficient books containing poems, stories and descriptions providing good visual and tactile imagery?
Has the teacher a rich collection of poetry and prose to encourage children to visualise?

6 THE POTENTIAL OF ART IN RELATION TO THE WHOLE CURRICULUM

Art experience should enable children to learn, organise, communicate, express and celebrate, using intuitive as well as logical processes. Its cross-curricular relevance should be seen as fundamental (in the same way as language, and hearing) rather than simply as illustrative of a skill-based link.

If projects and topics could be seen as multi-disciplined approaches, and investigations of equal importance, instead of forced integrations, the educational experience provided for children would be much enhanced. In some cases, sensory exploration of subject matter might lead to art forms and later into words, movement, dance, drama, mathematical or scientific studies; in others, a mathematical or scientific approach – or one from another discipline – might prove appropriate for the initial response. In any event, all aspects should be seen to be of equal value (although of varying balance, according to the requirements of the project).

Careful consideration needs to be given to the terminology we use, as this clarifies our own predispositions (which are often communicated to children unconsciously!). Is this plant study art or science? How we have distorted the natural wholeness of the experience if we can even ask this question, and how it would have puzzled our great botanical artists! Clearly, there will be times when the drawing is analytic – but it is still a drawing. At other times we may select and develop characteristics which will express qualities of the living flower, or its growth. In the best botanical illustrations, drawing has served many purposes, and the value of this challenge lies in the mutual benefit of both disciplines.

QUESTIONS
Is there sufficient time and flexibility in the timetable for the development of art in its own right?
Is art seen as a positive component in the balance of project work?
Does art generate work in other disciplines?
Do other disciplines generate work in art? If so, is the nature of the art experience in this context of real educational value?
Is art considered as a means of investigation and learning in: environmental studies? studies of artforms and artefacts?
If model-making is undertaken, is the process of real value in understanding the subject matter, or could a different approach be of more value – for example relief, painting, collage? Are the materials used close in character to the original stimuli?

Teaching

Having taken into consideration environment, organisation and resources, teachers may well question to what extent they should overtly teach art or perhaps 'just let it happen'. Clearly unless there are inviting materials and tools, very little work of value will be generated, therefore the organisation of these aspects can be seen as an integral part of teaching. Thus, when children seem spontaneously to research, communicate or express themselves in the context of a school with lively attitudes to learning and an interesting environment, it should be recognised for what it is – successful teaching (the hidden curriculum?). No doubt the teacher will build on these initiatives through the strategies of encouragement, appropriate resources – including time – and questioning designed to trigger thinking.

We consider children's symbolic imagery to be sacrosanct in early years in so far as it is personally evolved, and therefore teacher intervention is inappropriate. Overt teaching should take the form of encouragement to investigate the world, especially through visual and tactile means. The fact that the child may well respond in symbolic renderings offers valuable insight into the stage of development reached, and will enable the teacher to extend experience appropriately.

Teaching children to look and see, touch and feel, and to enjoy imagery through sensory experience and words should be an ongoing challenge from the first days in school to the day the child leaves. The whole 'input' of experience should be seen as a foundation for later response rather than as direct 'cause' and 'effect' in the short term.

Skills can be taught and will at times need to be quite specific, as, for instance, the appropriate use of adhesives, brushes, cutting tools and care of materials. The discipline of understanding classroom organisation – where things are kept and how they are cleaned and cared for – is important if children are to be enabled to work confidently and well. In extending experience of techniques it is often expedient to use the vehicle of an experimental period or 'game' where the children are challenged to find out what tools can do or how materials behave (always bearing safe practice in mind, of course).

For example, taking a graphic tool, challenge the children to cover their surface (of appropriate scale for the tool or material chosen) as quickly as they can with all kinds of scribble and markmaking.

See if you can change the paper (or other surface) so that it is mainly dark rather than light . . . ?
How many different patches of shade can you make?
How many different kinds of mark can you make?
How many different kinds of line?
Can you use marks and shades on top of one another?

This same challenge can be used with other tools and media, and, in later stages, with combinations. It is valuable to generate a certain amount of urgency in the time allocated to the experience – although the initial five or ten minutes challenge often needs to be extended as momentum is built up. Discussion of the gathered work as to who has managed to use the most shades; made the darkest, or lightest mark . . . enables the children to see new possibilities and to select qualities. The value of the exercise lies in developing understanding of the nature and possibilities offered by the tools and materials – benefits which may well be apparent in later work.

Possible tools or materials (used singly or in any combination) might be: pencils, chalk, charcoal, conté, pens and ink, brush and ink etc; paint, inks, collage, dough, clay.

The whole area of colour experience can be developed and extended using a similar approach (see page 52). A very real way of teaching can take the form of challenges to find out how a single colour or pair of colours behaves when used in different ways, 'How many can you make/find? . . . Do you think anyone will be able to? . . . What happens if . . . ? can offer a goal to aim for, a target to beat, or a problem to solve. It is good for teachers to join in these 'games' practically; by doing so they do not risk influencing the child's mode of image making.

These experimental games are an excellent precursor to specific open-ended challenges using the same tools and materials (other than for very young children who often need no such challenge).

Conversation during work often serves to extend the child's concentration period by rekindling interest in the reality of the experience. The child will sometimes develop ideas verbally which he began to discover through his art. When children reach points of difficulty, or lose confidence in their work, teachers may find it useful to concentrate on enabling the child to re-experience a 'happening' or, where relevant, to look once more or be 'talked around' the item or idea of interest. As the work proceeds, and at points where the child is not too deeply engrossed, the teacher will be intent on drawing the child out rather than feeding in ideas. There may well be a time during or at the end of a session, where looking at the positive aspects which have evolved in the children's work can be beneficial. There are very few, if any, pieces of work which have been undertaken with involvement, where some constructive and worthwhile comment cannot be made. The good teacher will build from interest and strength. Destructive criticism has no place in art education.

In this context templates, photographs, and the teacher's own drawing are all blind alleys; they offer inappropriate imagery which builds up the child's belief that he can only do it himself when he has something to copy. Use of these 'crutches' causes considerable problems in later stages of art education as the child's critical faculty has been distorted, as well as his own imagery being allowed to atrophy.

Direct teaching should be apparent in situations where the individual or groups of children are enabled to discuss their own work, as well as artefacts and forms of all kinds, in an open and fearless way. Enabling children to build up a variety of criteria for judgement, and building up confidence to enable consideration of what has been achieved or what proved difficult, is a very important aspect of art education.

Evaluation

Self-evaluation must be a high priority for any teacher. In assessing the effectiveness of personal practice careful consideration must be given to the question of the educational worth of experiences offered to the children.

In this context the following questions may prove useful:

1 *Are the children fully involved, absorbed and enthusiastic – if not, why not?*
2 *Was the stimulus appropriate, with a large proportion of first-hand experience?*
3 *Were the tools and materials adequate and well organised?*
4 *Is the work vigorous and well carried out, showing development of skills and techniques?*
5 *Is the child's response original, creative, inventive, or did the teacher take too much part in the problem solving?*
6 *Is there appropriate development in the work of each child over a period of time?*

The need to look at times at a sequence of work from one child is crucial if genuine consideration of development is to be achieved. This may well necessitate keeping a body of work in school, rather than sending it home at the end of the day. Implications regarding the teacher's performance are to be recognised by poor motivation, sterile imagery, poor quality in the use of materials and lack of interest and development on the part of the child.

All children have latent potential and imagination, which can only be developed and nurtured through a lively and practical programme based on visual and tactile experience and ideas. Teachers who believe that their pupils have no imagination, interest or gift need to consider their own understanding and teaching strategies.

It is important to maintain the fine balance between fostering and developing natural motivation and ability, and introducing and extending experience and skills (see Figure 3.1).

Figure 3.1

		TEACHER
	NATURAL MOTIVATION AND DRIVE	FOSTERS AND ENCOURAGES
	ABILITY TO USE SENSES. INTELLIGENCE, LOGIC, INTUITION.	PROVIDES FIRST HAND STIMULI. CHALLENGES TO SEE, TO FEEL (TOUCH). ENCOURAGES INITIATIVE, ANALYSIS AND EXPERIMENTATION
CHILD	ABILITY TO FEEL EMOTIONALLY TO ADMIRE, LOVE, HATE, DISLIKE, WONDER	PROVIDES STIMULI. NATURAL AND MAN-MADE, ART AND DESIGN FORMS, FROM ALL TIMES AND CULTURES: ALSO IN THE FORM OF WORDS, POEMS, PROSE, SONG, MUSIC, MOVEMENT, DRAMA. ENCOURAGES PERSONAL RESPONSE
	ABILITY TO REMEMBER	TRIGGERS AND ENCOURAGES 'RE EXPERIENCE' AND RECALL
	PREDISPOSITION TO RESPOND TO MATERIALS, TO ARRANGE AND RE-ARRANGE, TO ORDER, TO EXPERIMENT, TO PLAY.	SUPPLIES APPROPRIATE TOOLS AND MATERIALS. ENCOURAGES EXPERIMENTATION AND ENJOYMENT. FOSTERS THE ABILITY TO SEE POSSIBILITIES AND THE DEVELOPMENT OF IDEAS. TEACHES RESPECT AND RESPONSIBILITY FOR TOOLS AND MATERIALS.

Chapter 4 The Art Curriculum

'A curriculum in art needs sufficient continuity so that skills can be developed, refined, and internalized and hence become a part of an expressive repertoire'

Eliot Eisner

NOTHING WE WRITE here is intended to devalue intuitive, spontaneous work. The ability to respond with insight to the needs of the children and to the opportunities of the moment is the hallmark of a good teacher, and there can be no opposition between such flexibility and overall planning. Many unexpected activities can contribute towards the achievement of such objectives.

Sequential and developmental planning is essential and should consist of three elements.

1 *Learning activities* These will provide the child with experiences to encourage creative development of ideas for expression. Perceptional and tactile sensitivity is increased by learning to organise complex information, and becoming confident in handling tools and materials. Contemplative experience of art and design forms can also be included under this heading.

2 *Self-directed activities* Here, children are given opportunity to exercise their ability to make choices and act upon them at their own pace.

3 *Integral activities* In these, art is seen as an integral part of a whole and is used to complement, and be complemented by, other curriculum areas.

Overall aims for the art curriculum can be defined as follows.

- to develop exploratory inventive thought and action, and the ability to innovate, initiate, discriminate and make effective personal responses;
- to develop visual and tactile sensitivity, and powers of observation, together with awareness of colour, form and space in the environment, and the manmade world;
- to develop understanding of a variety of media and processes in order to record, communicate and express ideas and feelings in many different ways;
- to develop non-verbal means of organising ideas, and seeing relationships which supplement and reinforce verbal learning;
- to develop understanding of modes of thought, expression and communication through visual and tactile means;
- to develop imagination, feeling and sensibility.

There is a crucial need to analyse a stage by stage development for building up a sound art curriculum. We have therefore devised a method using three phases which may prove to be a useful starting point for further individual and school development.

Stage 1 Offers *a diagram showing a broad, balanced art education structure*. This can be used as an introductory checklist for the individual, or the whole school staff in order to assess the breadth of present practice.

Stage 2 offers a diagram as a *foundation for developmental curriculum planning*.

Stage 3 expands on the particular nature and contribution of the areas of experience in drawing, painting, colour, printmaking, collage, textiles, three-dimensional work, response to artefacts, and design.

Stage 1: Initial checklist

This initial checklist can be used when considering breadth of experience in the basic areas of two- and three-dimensional work.

Pencil, chalk, wax, crayons, pens, brushes	DRAWING
Powder, Tempera, Poster, Inks, natural pigments etc.	PAINTING
Potato and other vegetables, card, wood, string, miscellaneous	PRINTMAKING
Paper, card, fabric, threads and fibres, feathers, wood, metal, polystyrene etc.	COLLAGE
Threads, fibres, fabrics. (Woven, knotted, patterned, dyed, embroidered, etc.)	TEXTILES
Clay, plasticine, dough, junk, modelling, wood, polystyrene, sculpture, etc.	THREE DIMENSIONAL
Displays, visits, objects, drawings, paintings, sculpture, reproductions, etc.	RESPONSE TO ARTEFACTS (own and other)

AGE	GENERAL PATTERN OF DEVELOPMENT	OBJECTIVES	INPUT	VOCABULARY
4 YEARS	Abstract scribble and pattern. Rich use of media and material. (Mainly based on a kinaesthetic response). Some representation of symbols emerging.	To build up confidence and enjoyment in the use of tools and materials in a lively and dynamic way. To foster willingness/eagerness to explore a variety of basic tools (including the hands) and materials, and to enable the children to use them with confidence. To build up experience through seeing, touching and doing.	Encouraging use of the senses to their fullest extent. Introducing a wide variety of natural and man made objects. Enabling experience of environment. Introducing basic tools and materials, songs, stories, poems, music, etc.	Mainly 'doing' words – painting, drawing, printing, modelling, scratching, pressing etc. Naming tools and materials. Response words – nice, nasty, etc. Scale words – big, small, etc. Naming colours.
5 YEARS	Build up of symbols often alongside 'scribble' experience and experiment. Figures, self, houses, trees, animals, flowers, machinery, etc. The simple forms and constructions are sometimes named. Enjoyment of colour, pattern and form in their own right. Personal value regarding scale. Shapes are seldom overlapped. Involvement in role play with 2 and 3 dimensional work.	To build up confidence in approach to new situations, tools and materials. To motivate communication and expression of personal ideas.	Introducing different tools and materials, fostering awareness of their qualities and care. Making collections. Setting up interest tables and displays. Introducing stories, songs, poems, descriptions, paintings, drawings, models and artefacts past and present.	Describing colours. Understanding organisational words. Descriptive words based on touching, looking and feelings – hard, soft, rough, smooth, cold, warm, happy, sad etc. Discussion of art and design forms. Generating new vocabulary.
6–7 YEARS	Apparent need for selected detail. Imagery developing into a means for expressing and communicating ideas, happenings, imaginings and stories. Growing desire to analyse and to make likenesses. Joy in pattern, colour, texture and form. For some children apparent need for visual realism.	To generate work showing a personal response to experience. To foster an inventive and lively attitude together with the ability to persevere through problems to a conclusion. To build up experience of tools and materials and to extend expectation of the nature of art. To foster visual and tactile discrimination and awareness.	Introducing a wide variety of natural and man made items, supported by visits and excursions linked with all curriculum areas. Building up personal collections, objects, pictures, etc. Introducing a variety of ways of experiencing, observing and responding. Generating discussion.	Extension of colour vocabulary. Linking colours to items – raspberry, pillar box, etc. Organisational words. Repeat, overlap, symmetry, regular, irregular, etc. Words describing visual and tactile qualities and feelings. Description of artefacts. Discussion.
8–9 YEARS	Use of symbolism and analysis. Interest in dramatic happenings and everyday life. Fascination for detail and sections of things as well as whole views. Narrative drawings and paintings. Interest in designing working models and build-up of techniques.	To build up a vocabulary of practical experience with special attention to working from first hand stimuli. To foster the ability to recognise and discuss different approaches to their own and other peoples work. To consider the nature of design. To develop listening and reading skills.	Considering and discussing art and design forms past and present and the reasons for their creation. Initiating visits to galleries and museums. Introducing artists and craftsmen and designers into school. Introducing projects involving art, design, music, movement and drama. Developing group projects and challenges, encouraging ability to plan, work as a team and deal with the challenges of co-operation. Encouraging involvement of working at home – sketchbooks, collections etc.	Understanding the meaning of matching, dark and light, hot and cold colours, hues, shades, contrasts. Technical items used in processes. Naming techniques and tools – sculpture, modelling, weaving, hanging, pottery, relief, construction, manuscript, calligraphy, print, engraving etc. Building up listening and reading skills needed in order to understand challenges and problems. Fostering ability to organise words to plan, annotate and describe some design processes.
10–11 YEARS	Personal statements and responses to challenge. Environmental work. Recording, analysing, expressing and communicating. Interest in scale/proportion, and spatial qualities. Evidence of experience in handling media, materials and tools.	To consider challenges (self imposed or other) and to respond to them, selecting appropriate tools and materials. Working through problems. To have some understanding of the nature and possibilities of art and design experience.		

COLOUR (pigment – paint, inks, dyes etc.)	PATTERN (Painted, printed, dyed, rubbed, imprinted, embossed, etc.)	TEXTURE (collage, threads, fibres, fabrics, surfaces, wood, clay, etc.)	FORM (3 dimensional experience, rigid and malleable materials.)	DRAWING (pencils, chalk, pen, brushes, fingers, etc.)	DESIGNING (2 and 3 dimension) spontaneous and planned.	RESPONSE TO ARTEFACTS & Design Forms.
Experiencing and using colour. Naming: (Presentation of of pigments, mixed by the teacher but varying in colour range and hue from time to time.	Non figurative paintings, drawings, printing, imprinting, collage etc.	Handling, manipulating and enjoying using materials. Sensory experience.	Handling, feeling, enjoying and manipulating materials. Constructing. Building and destroying. Sensory experience.	Markmaking. Enjoyment of using graphic tools, fingers, hands, chalk, pens, pencils, brushes.	Building on all areas of experience. Play and spontaneous experiment with materials and tools. Building and taking apart. Collections – Sorting. Talking.	Introduction of art and design forms of all kinds. Talking. Likes and dislikes. Personal response.
Collections of colour. Sorting, selecting, describing. Mixing.	Awareness of surface patterns. Rubbings. Experiment. Arrangements of natural and man made items.	Awareness of surface texture and the feel of different qualities. Collecting, sorting, rubbing, discussing. Collage and construction	Use of hands and tools. Random forms. Embodiment of personal ideas. Constructions, assemblages, junk, dolls, puppets etc.	Experimenting with a wide range of tools, materials and surfaces. Embodying ideas and building up ways of representing their own world and experience.	Growing awareness of tools and materials – Characteristics and qualities. Development of skills in relation to purposes. Personal problem solving. Talk, draw, write about ideas.	Paintings, drawings, print, sculpture models, ceramics, textiles, buildings, machinery and design forms – Enjoyment and discussion.
Awareness of the variety and qualities of colour in the environment. Looking at pictures and artefacts. Discussing. Matching.	Experimenting, arranging, folding repeating, overlapping. Regular and irregular patterning. Looking at patterns. Discussing	Responding to materials. Arranging and re-arranging. Developing into pattern, relief and pictures. Dolls, puppets. Destruction of materials to learn qualities. Construction and reconstruction.	Awareness of natural and man made forms and environments. Modelling, Building hand pots. Expression of personal experiences and ideas Discussing.	Growing aware-ness of natural and man made environment. Analysing, expressing and communicating personal interest and feelings pertaining to it. Looking at drawings. Working out ideas through drawing. Discussion.	Evolving new ideas – modifying and testing where relevant. Spontaneous making, and talking about possibilities. Thinking about function.	Visits, excursions in the neighbour-hood and further afield. Artists, designers and craftsmen in school. Original works and reproductions.
Mixing and matching. Using colour to express and describe. Discussing.	Searching for pattern. Using the environment and other sources. Recording, rubbing, printing, analysing.	Awareness of the nature of materials and surfaces. Discussion of surface decoration – Pots, models, etc. Using to express and communicate ideas.	Understanding the qualities and potential of constructional and malleable materials as a means of problem solving. Expression. Construction: forms, models, buildings etc. Clay: slabbing and coiling. Extending techniques in relation to ideas.	Analysis of qualities – shape, line, pattern, form and texture in the environment. Fantasy ideas. Using drawing as a means of designing.	Broad skill development. Personal or group thinking. Problem solving. Emphasis on ways of working and process. Awareness of alternatives and options, and of how to gather information. Ability to isolate problems.	Museums and galleries. Looking at functional design. Discussing the ways in which things were made – colour, form, technique.
Controlling and experimenting. Particular qualities of tone, shades, hue and mood. Considering colour for purposes. Expressing through colour. Discussing	Organising pattern. Using shape. Abstract pattern. Expressing mood. Pattern for purposes. (Book covers, curtains, dolls and puppets, clothes, boxes, folders etc.)	Awareness of the potential of the uses of material. Use of found and constructed textures in expressive and analytical work, and design.	Understanding adhesives, and methods of construction. Investigating, analysing and interpreting natural and man made forms and environments. Considering light, and shadow, form and space.	Awareness of dark and light, form and texture. Awareness of the potential of tools and materials appropriate to embody ideas and serve needs.	Awareness of the vital relationship between the natural and man made world (conservation). Logical and intuitive ways of working. Enjoying the functional and expressive qualities of materials. Personal collections, sketch and note books. Beginning to sequence and predict.	Development of interest in differing modes of communication and expression. Form and function, personal enjoyment and response.

Stage 3: The nature and contribution of areas of experience

> **DRAWING**
>
> Graphic tools, brushes, printing and imprinting equipment.

Drawing is a fundamental activity in its own right; it has been a mode of communicating and expression throughout the ages. In educating children it also has a strong contribution to make in the learning process, with its inherent possibilities for deepening understanding through intensive looking, selection and organisation of visual matter.

Drawing begins in the accidental – then experimental – scribble and mark-making of the pre-school child. In early stages it is of paramount importance to offer a variety of tools and materials, taking care to see that the basic range for graphic needs is always available. Introducing ever-new media, to the exclusion of materials and tools the child has used before, can lead to a superficial sampling, lack of mastery and preclusion of self-rewarding experience.

It is a fallacy that the young child will only respond to large tools and pieces of paper. Though many do, others are inhibited by this approach. It has been found that some children (even those with problems of manual dexterity) responded to fine line tools such as fibre tips and biro pens. Hence both extremes of scale should be introduced. As the child is given opportunity to use graphic tools – pencils, pens, brushes, crayons, chalks etc, the drawings develop into a means of organising and communicating personal experiences. Communication is seldom overtly aimed at others but has more to do with gathering visual information, and selecting and organising it in various ways – a kind of 'thinking aloud'.

For the young child drawing should be strongly biased towards subjective experience and response, but regard should also be paid to the objective component. In the early stages this will be directed toward observing and touching; it is up to the teacher to surround the children with interesting natural and manmade items. The response will be apparent in the enrichment of symbolism and motivation to investigate other areas of reality and experience.

As signs of an analytic response become apparent, children can be challenged to observe intensely and to work from the basis of direct experience of the natural and manmade world, celebrating it with a variety of tools and materials selected for the purpose. The child should be challenged to look, touch and think before drawing. This kind of stimulus helps to build a visual vocabulary which in turn feeds the imagination. Media experimentation can run alongside intense searching, and the two approaches can offer mutually beneficial aspects of the drawing experience (see page 155: Drawing project).

Drawing can also be used as a means of planning other kinds of work – designing, and organising ideas. However, it is of little value as a precursor to working in other materials if the child does not have experience of the qualities and nature of material to be used. For example, a child who draws a castle to be executed in sand will face disappointment and failure unless he also understands the potential and limitations of sand as a building material. Designs for work in clay or printmaking can be equally difficult to transpose from a drawing, moreover, this approach fails to offer children valuable experience of the unique qualities and accidental possibilities of working directly with the material. Results of this way of working are often characterised by a lack of vigour and liveliness.

Where a child *does* have experience of tools and materials, drawing and designing can become a kind of shorthand, a means whereby ideas can be developed before translation into a final form. Challenging children to draw items they have already made can lead to some interesting results. These drawings can be especially valuable in understanding the nature of designing where the child attempts to record the processes of work leading to a pattern, pot, model, book, etc.

Problem solving as a function of drawing comes into its own with children around the age of eight or nine years. They can be challenged to make drawings to show how things work, to invent, to plan and to modify. At this stage children also enjoy devising diagrams and maps. Pattern-making in all its forms can be developed alongside children's increasing awareness of line, shape and tone.

Many different kinds of drawing should be discussed, including original work by the children or adults, reproductions from all themes and cultures, children's book illustrations and plans and working drawings (architect's and designer's for example).

If we have enabled children to understand and use the powerful tool of drawing by the time they leave the primary school, they are likely to see it right across the secondary curriculum in both science and arts disciplines.

Note It was interesting to note that in some schools children considering a number of drawings showed some surprise that they were considered 'finished', as they had not been 'coloured in'. This led to some thought on the part of the teachers regarding the 'expectation' they had engendered.

'French horn'
Pencil and crayon drawing. Girl.

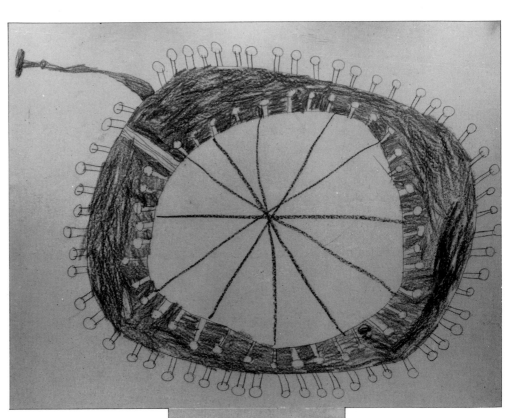

Suzanne   19.3.4.
the French horn
Was like a great big
hole in the road
and if there Was one
the cars and lorries
and motor - bikes and
bikes
Wouldn't be able to ride
there.

Pencil pattern. Girl. 8 years. 165 × 185 mms.

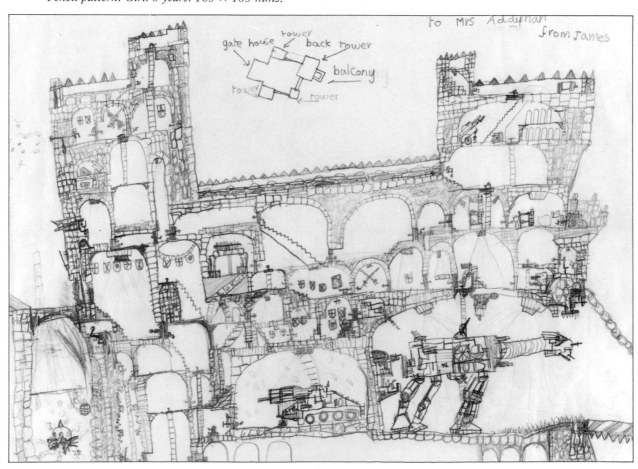

Castle. Boy. 10 years. Pencil. 210 × 295 mms.

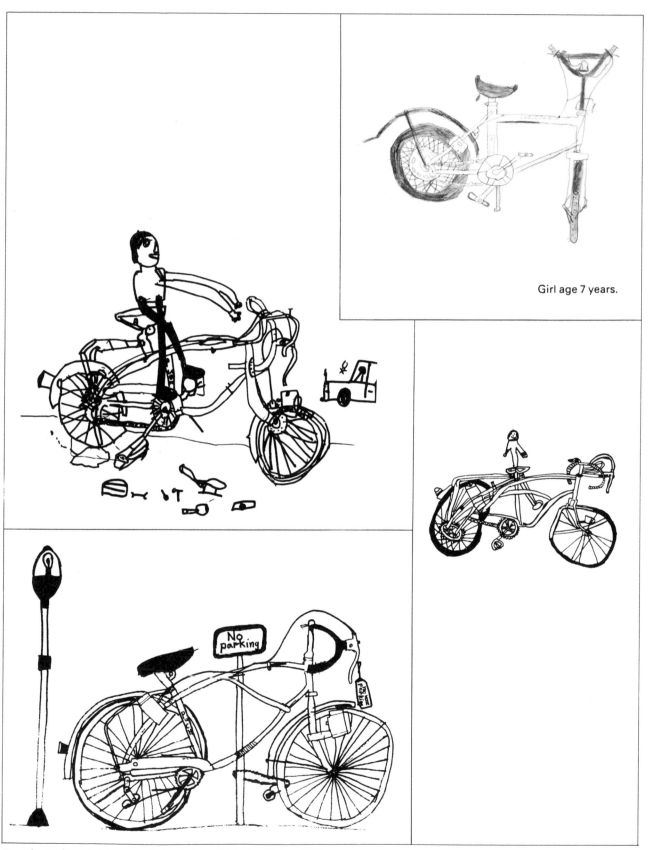

Girl age 7 years.

Bicycle studies. 7–10 years. Paint, ink and felt tip. 210 × 295 mms.

Direct drawings. Pen and ink. 8–10 years. 295 cms × 210 cms.

After a visit by musicians. Boy. 6 years. 150 × 190 mms.

Suffolk Church. Boy. 7 years. Felt tip. 210 × 145 mms.

Man in a Bath. 9 years. Pencil, crayon and felt tip. 240 × 330 mms.

'Cat' (study from an animal brought into the classroom). Girl. 10 years. Chalk and charcoal.
435 × 95 mms.

Plant study. Girl 11 years. White powder colour on black sugar paper. 470 × 360 mms.

DRAWING

Basic materials and tools

It is suggested that the colours are limited to blacks, whites, ochres and browns
at times in order to concentrate the childrens' attention on graphic qualities.

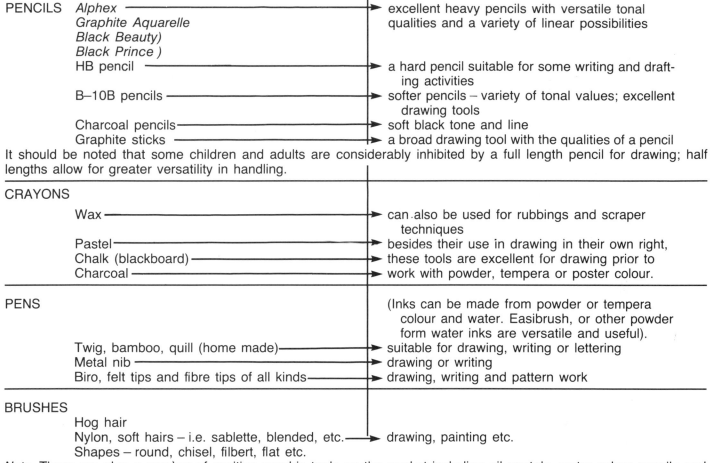

PENCILS *Alphex* ——————————————→ excellent heavy pencils with versatile tonal
        Graphite Aquarelle   qualities and a variety of linear possibilities
        Black Beauty)
        Black Prince)
        HB pencil ——————————————→ a hard pencil suitable for some writing and draft-
                                         ing activities
        B–10B pencils ——————————→ softer pencils – variety of tonal values; excellent
                                         drawing tools
        Charcoal pencils——————————→ soft black tone and line
        Graphite sticks ——————————→ a broad drawing tool with the qualities of a pencil

It should be noted that some children and adults are considerably inhibited by a full length pencil for drawing; half
lengths allow for greater versatility in handling.

CRAYONS

        Wax ——————————————→ can also be used for rubbings and scraper
                                         techniques
        Pastel——————————————→ besides their use in drawing in their own right,
        Chalk (blackboard) ————————→ these tools are excellent for drawing prior to
        Charcoal ——————————————→ work with powder, tempera or poster colour.

PENS

                                         (Inks can be made from powder or tempera
                                         colour and water. Easibrush, or other powder
                                         form water inks are versatile and useful).
        Twig, bamboo, quill (home made)———→ suitable for drawing, writing or lettering
        Metal nib ——————————————→ drawing or writing
        Biro, felt tips and fibre tips of all kinds———→ drawing, writing and pattern work

BRUSHES
        Hog hair
        Nylon, soft hairs – i.e. sablette, blended, etc.——→ drawing, painting etc.
        Shapes – round, chisel, filbert, flat etc.

Note There are also a number of exciting graphic tools on the market including oil pastels, water colour pencils and
sticks.

COLOUR
Paint, inks, dyestuffs, crayons, pastel, threads and fibres, collage materials, textiles etc.

Early colour experience will include playing with materials, collecting, sorting, arranging, rearranging and generally enjoying the diverse qualities of colour. Colour is a vibrant and exciting experience engendering a warm response, provided that the teacher offers appropriate stimulus, tools, materials and pigments.

Paint should be richly mixed, in a consistency which does not drip down the paper when applied. Appropriate containers, mixing palettes, and good quality hog hair and soft brushes should be offered to the children. Graphic tools of all kinds should be of good quality, enabling strong even marks. Paper should be varied and appropriate to the task in hand. Organisation of materials should preclude accidents and offer easy access. Children should be encouraged to collect and put away tools and materials in a habitual and disciplined way from an early age. The position of work when painting will vary, depending on the challenge in hand. Table tops, floor, easels, boards and wall surface will all be suitable on some occasions.

Colours should be identified and named as early as possible, introducing primary and secondary colours – red, blue, yellow, purple, green and orange, with the addition of black, white, grey and brown and other hues – as deemed appropriate and relevant. In the nursery and reception stages, the teacher will mix, or be responsible for the supervision of mixing paint for the children. It is important to see that a range of the basic colours is available and that at times the children are offered alternative mixtures – differently mixed greens, purples, oranges, browns, greys etc – in order to extend experience and expectation. Clearly there will be times when children use one or two colours only or are limited to a restricted range.

As the children develop and gain experience, more control is apparent in their handling of paint and symbols begin to appear. It is important at this stage that children do not fall into the trap of seeing colour only as an infill to drawing. This can happen all too easily, as they will often have experience of 'colouring in' in other areas of the curriculum (for example, mathematics) and through painting books at home. Teacher and parent expectation can sometimes foster this to the extent that linear drawings are seen only as a vehicle for crayoning or painting.

At this stage the children should be encouraged to experiment with colour. Colour-mixing games offer almost endless possibilities and scope and can range from graphic tool play, to paint, collage, or mixed media experimentation. Working in pairs can stimulate discussion and build up children's confidence.

Starting points for colour mixing games might be:

- *What happens when you mix these* (provided) *colours? Are you sure those are all the colours you can make?*
- *See how many different colours/hues/shades/tints you can make from. . .*
  two or three primary colours
  primary colour + black
  primary colour + white
  one, two or three primary colours + black and white . . .
- Challenge the children to divide a large piece of sugar paper into shapes using a broad graphic tool, for example blackboard chalk, and paint the 'grid' produced in a variety of ways. This can extend colour experience in as simple, or sophisticated a way as is deemed appropriate. Favourite colours – magic patchwork quilts where all the colours are mixed; not using the same colour twice; using mood, seasonal or elemental colours – are but a few of the many possibilities.

Note Pencil drawing prior to using any kind of powder, poster or tempera paint is in general too restrictive, and is inappropriate for the broad, generous quality of the medium. Children who attempt to combine the two soon grow disappointed at the apparent loss of quality of their original shapes, and will resist painting. The fact that the broad line of brush, pastel or blackboard chalk at first seems less satisfactory to the child is partly explained by his need to see an 'acceptable' image at every stage of the work. To change his approach, encouragement and support on the part of the teacher will be necessary. A direct challenge to draw with other tools than the pencil, prior to painting, will prove more fruitful than precluding its use! Children may be interested to look at examples of work created in various ways – Chinese painters draw with brushes, cavemen used chalk and charcoal.

Colour theory of any kind is inappropriate in early years. Only when children are thoroughly conversant, practically, with the quality and variety of colour should the simplest kind of theory be touched upon. The child who has been taught the theory that red and yellow make orange may never understand that this is only a partial truth. Red and yellow will in fact make many kinds of orange, and the addition of small quantities of other colours, black and white, will not change it out of the orange range.

In early stages of painting, children may well use paint decoratively rather than representationally – faces may be blue, or tigers green. This is the stage when experimentation and enjoyment of colour can abound, and is the optimum period for practical learning about the qualities of colour. If used constructively, a wealth of experience can be built up, unhindered by the additional problems which will very soon loom, as the need for representational colour, followed by matching, becomes apparent. In fact this early experience may well provide the means for coming to terms with these later stages.

Children should continually be challenged to see subtlety and variety in colour. Displays could include an invitation for children to participate by bringing in items, or building colour 'environments' for themselves, or for toys and dolls. It may be possible to change the light in some part of the room, near the display or environment by covering a window with cellophane, using coloured light bulbs, or spotlights with gelatines. Colour 'spectacles' can be made to change the hue.

Attention should be drawn to myriad colours of the immediate environment, in both natural and manmade objects. Identification of contrasts – warm and cold, light and dark, happy and sad or mysterious colours, all add to the child's vocabulary and experience.

The ability to mix and match colour is a skill which can be built up as experience is gained. Resource materials including scraps of material and paper, dried and flattened leaves, bark etc, can be used as initial stimulus and children challenged to mix appropriate colours to match the items. Materials can be selected and arranged in transparent sweet jars, sorted into ranges of colour, or contrasts for possible matching challenges, or for experience in selection.

Introduction to transparent colour opens new vistas of experience. Dye stuffs, wax resists and flooding with transparent inks, overlaid tissues, nets and cellophane offer further variety.

Discussion could focus on different effects produced by using a variety of pigments and consistencies, tools and materials. The scale of graphic tools and brushes, and the size of marks made, will give differing visual effects. Painting colour against colour, using mixed media and collage, experimenting with graphic tools over or underlaying paint can extend to almost limitless possibilities in practice.

If experience is built up in this way, confidence and control of colour is apparent, and children will fearlessly experiment when faced with a problem, rather than relying on the teacher for direction.

Colour education can be enhanced from early years by the introduction of original works of art or craft – pictures, slides, books, textiles etc. The children can be invited to respond to colour, and led to consider ways in which artists have used it and the effects they have achieved. (The work of Colourists, Impressionists and Post

Impressionists, Expressionists, and artforms from Indian, Persian and Mexican cultures, for example, lend themselves especially well.) A totally new concept to many children is the way colours change and merge when viewed from different distances. This often has a bearing on the way in which they begin to make judgements about their own work.

Palettes

Children should be encouraged to mix paints as early as possible and will need palettes from the latter part of the reception year.

Circular infant sorting trays (white) are excellent. Purpose designed palettes; bun tins and biscuit tin lids (painted with household white undercoat and gloss). Unbreakable plates (melamine, or enamel) are also appropriate.

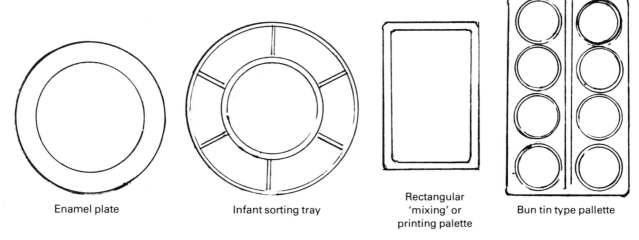

Enamel plate

Infant sorting tray

Rectangular 'mixing' or printing palette

Bun tin type pallette

Water Containers

The cleanliness of the water has a great deal to do with the quality of colour experience.

Containers should hold *at least a ½ pint of water*, should stack and be non-tipping.

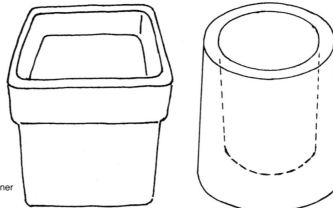

Purpose-made non-tipping, stackable water container

Food or ice-cream container (also stackable and non-tipping)

Paper

Newspaper (printed)	For brush drawings, collage and painting etc.
Newsprint	For brush drawings, rubbings, chalk, heavy pencil, wax, collage, etc.
Computer paper	Drawing with brush and graphic tools, rubbings, etc.
Sugar paper (various weights)	For drawing of all kinds with heavy graphic tools, brushes and ink/paint. Painting, collage, etc.
Bond paper/Bank paper	Lightweight and smooth surface papers for drawing, handwriting, etc.

Cartridge paper	Heavier quality white or cream paper for drawing, design, painting etc.
Brown paper (large sheets)	For murals, collage/paintings.

Brushes

Cheap brushes prove expensive in the long – or even short – term. The quality of work depends to a large extent on brushes available. Teachers should experiment with brushes to ensure that they are reasonable tools to enable purposeful work.

There should be a selection of various sized brushes so that each child has the opportunity to use two or three, if required, on a piece of work.

Hoghair brushes, soft hair brushes – nylon, sablette, etc.

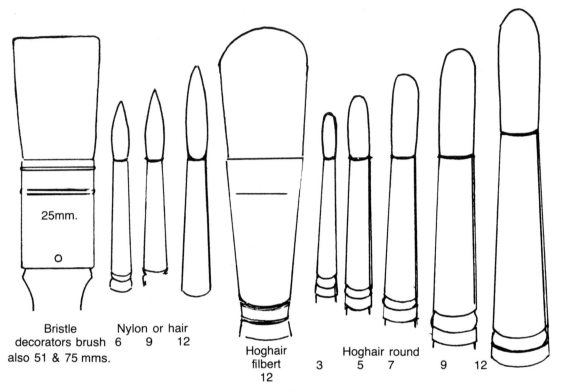

Bristle decorators brush also 51 & 75 mms.

Nylon or hair 6 9 12

Hoghair filbert 12

Hoghair round 3 5 7 9 12

Paint Containers

It is essential to choose containers large enough for the purpose, stackable and non-tipping.

Screw topped plastic jars set in containers are also useful, provided the container is of a reasonable size.

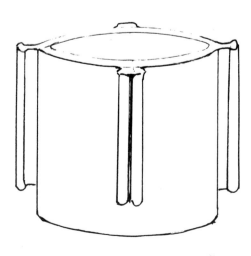

Actual size 2½″ (6 cms) × 2½″ (6 cms).

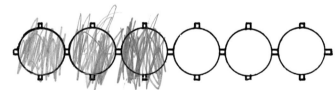

Arrangement allowing for covering tempera or poster colour with a 'water jacket', which can be poured off prior to use.

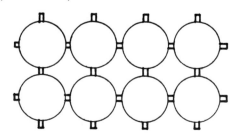

COLOUR

*Basic materials, tools and equipment

PAINT. It is crucial to the quality of the art experience, and to the way in which children learn to use and control colour that:
(a) the kind of paint chosen can be mixed thickly, and is rich enough in character to enable vibrant colours to be made;
(b) a full basic colour range is available so that purposeful colour mixing and matching is possible.

Powder, liquid tempera, and poster colour are all suitable. Water colour boxes, and tempera blocks are limited in their uses, and will not be appropriate for use as a basic range.

Basic colour range.   BLACK: WHITE: A COOL YELLOW (or lemon): A WARM YELLOW (or an ochre): SCARLET OR VERMILION: CRIMSON: A BRIGHT BLUE (or ultramarine): A GREENY BLUE (or Prussian).
If a green is required, a VIRIDIAN is useful, but from the basic yellows and blues, a variety of good greens are easily mixed.

(NOTE when ordering paint it is usual to need twice as much yellow and white pigment as the other colours.)

Owl Pencil and Conté drawing. 36 × 52 cms. Girl. 6 years.

Owl. Pencil and Conté drawing. 37 × 55 cms. Girl. 6 years.

'They threw snowballs all over me.' Powder Colour, wax crayon and chalk. 47 × 37 cms.
Girl. 6 years.

Bird
Sequence of 3 paintings. Girl. 7 years.

Sunbathing. Girl. 9 years. Paint, wax and collage. 48 × 35 cms.

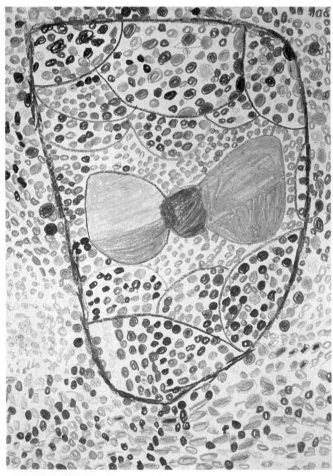

My Smartie Easter Egg. Girl. 6 years. Wax crayon. 250 × 200 mms.

Vase of Flowers. Girl. 10 years.
Powder colour. 57 × 47.5 cms.

Man with his arms full of stars. Girl 10 years.
Powder colour and pastel. 57 × 47.5 cms.

What I'd like to be. Girl. 8 years. 60 × 48 cms.

N. American Indian Mask. Girl. 10 years.

Nigerian Head. Girl. 6 years.

Painting of head after Paul Klee.

Painting of head after Augustus John. Girl. 10 years.

After looking at Impressionist paintings. Girl. 10 years.

After Van Gogh flowers. Girl. 10 years.

Colour matching challenge. 10 years. A section of a colour supplement picture forms the original challenge to match and extend.

66

Lovely sky. Boy. 8 years.

Road near the school

The Giant running after Jack. Powder Colour and Chalk.
Girl. 5 years. 42 × 59 cms.

Pop Group. Powder Colour painting. Boy. 11 years 56 × 41 cms.

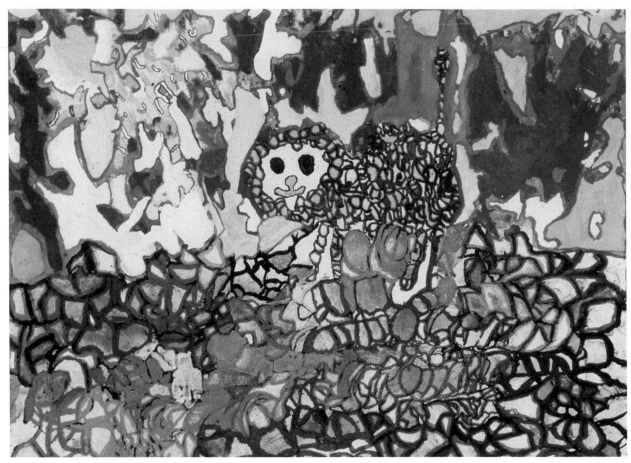

'Lion'. Boy. 9 years. Print and paint. 375 × 500 mms

'Devil in the Sky'. Boy. 9 years. Print and paint and chalk. 375 × 500 mms

Pig in a maze. Print and Paint. Boy. 8 years. 37 × 50 cms.

Self portrait. Pastel Drawing. Boy. 11 years. 48 × 29 cms.

Girl. 10 years. Textile collage.

Hilltop Road. Boy. 9 years. Wool collage on paper. 29 × 31 cms.

> **PRINTMAKING**
> Potato and other vegetables, junk, polystyrene, card, string, wood, clay, lino, monoprints from flat surfaces loaded with pigments etc.

Printmaking is a rich source of pleasure, learning and expression. It is based on pattern making with particular emphasis on shape, line and colour. It can also be used as a means of drawing, especially (but not exclusively) interesting for children with problems of manipulation in dealing with graphic tools.

Early experiences begin with random experimental printing using hands, feet, vegetables, cork, cotton reels and junk of all descriptions, with paint or inks loaded on to flat surfaces. It is sometimes advisable to limit children to the use of one strong colour, or black, to begin with. This encourages inventive use of the 'block' and the build up of complex images rather than a series of single prints in ever-changing colour. Thick paint with a squeeze of washing-up liquid, or water-based printing inks are suitable for the purpose. Foam or flannel pads on flat 'plates' or printing rollers can be used for loading the 'blocks'. Newspaper, newsprint, computer paper and scrap material afford excellent surfaces for all experimental printwork.

As the child gains confidence, experience and manual dexterity a number of challenges can be introduced, and prints can progress from simple forms to highly sophisticated patterns and designs. Such challenges might include:

- making a variety of repeating patterns, random or organised – spots, stripes, edge to edge, rotated, spiral, radiating, drops and half drops, etc
- building up repeating patterns into overlapped shapes and colours, making more complex motifs
- building up printed patterns, adding and overlaying paint, collage, and graphic materials
- making symmetrical and asymmetrical patterns
- using print to 'draw' from first-hand experience. Work can be enriched and embellished with graphic tools, oil pastels, transparent inks, and paint, etc
- researching the surface patterns of birds, animals, fish, bark etc. and analysing them in print form, as well as building up drawings of whole, or parts of items
- imprinting into clay, dough, plasticine, and embellishing with found items (clay cannot be fired in this condition)
- printing on fabrics and other surfaces and embellishing with stitchery, collage etc
- designing prints for fabrics, book jackets, decorative panels etc
- building up 'paintings' in thick ink or pigment on a flat surface, taking prints, and replenishing/modifying the original surface before reprinting (working into the prints)

Any experimental prints which are of no further use, make excellent collage material when torn up and added to the bit box!

Resources

Flat surfaces (formica, tiling, etc)
Tiles, plates, linoleum etc
Foam sheeting, flannel, etc (printing pads)
Wood, lino, polystyrene etc (blocks)
Powder or tempera colours
Water colour printing inks
Printing rollers (4″/10 cm)
Palette knives
Adhesives (strong enough to fix items to blocks for printing, eg PVA)
Collections of found objects, threads, fibres, fabrics, card, etc
Variety of paper and materials for printing

Rolling ink on to a 'Press Print' block.

Tree study. Girl. 9 years.
Black powder colour.
370 × 250 mms.

'Lots of Sheep.' Girl.
4 years. Rubbings.
280 × 370 cms.

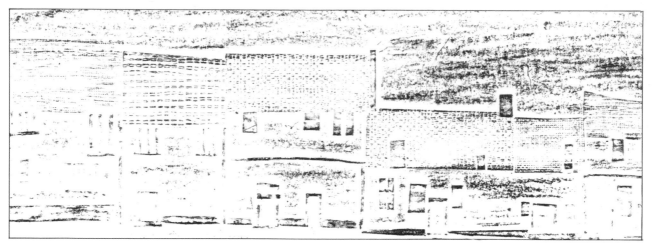

'Village Street'. Girl. 10 years. Card and Wallpaper collage rubbing, (following a school expedition). 215 × 600 mms.

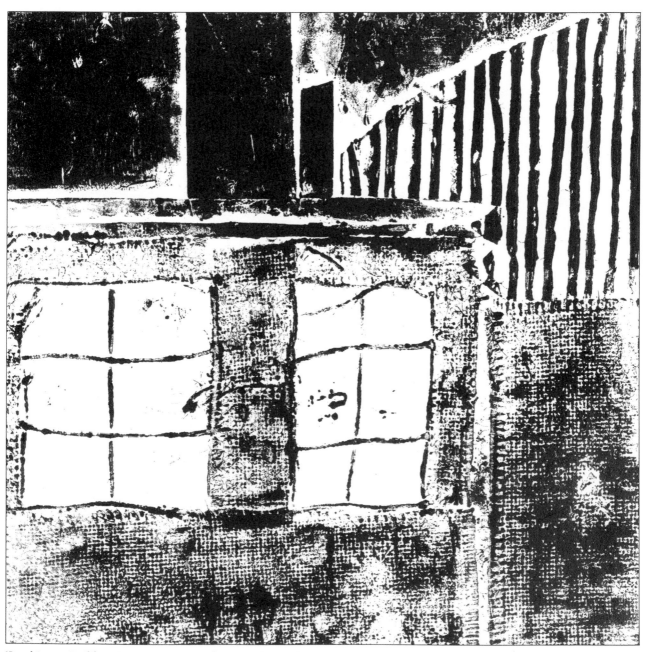

'Looking at Buildings'. Boy 11+. Found items. 180 × 185 mms.

> **COLLAGE**
> No self-respecting classroom should be without a richly-resourced 'bit' box or bag!
> — *threads and fibres, fabric of all kinds, papers, card, wood, metal, stone, found objects, leather, fur, feathers, grasses, reeds, straws, leaves, buttons, sequins etc.*
> — *a variety of adhesives*

Collage is an effective and useful activity which provides a link between visual and tactile experience. It can be used as a vehicle for analytic, expressive or communicative work. It is especially useful in building up an understanding of composition and design, as a number of different arrangements can be worked through prior to finalising by sticking or fixing in other ways. A wide range of materials should be available, which will provide a variety of colour, texture and shape. The richness or poverty of the experience will depend on provision of basic raw material from which children can select.

Early activity will embrace selecting, sorting, discussing, tearing and sticking. Cutting can be introduced as soon as manipulative abilities make it possible. As the child develops, more complex activities can be introduced, including cutting and sewing, using paper, fabrics, yarns and threads, and working with card, wood, plastics and found objects. Provided an immediate 'end product' is not set by the teacher as an explicit or implicit goal, there is much scope for learning in the process of building a collage.

Children should be encouraged to play sorting games, grouping items into 'families' of visual or tactile qualities: colour, tone, mood, warmth and cold, seasons etc; qualities of touch – rough, smooth, shiny, dull; items which suggest a character; sorting according to personal likes and dislikes; all these will help build up skills of selection and discrimination. No actual 'end product' is necessary unless a collection lends itself to development or finalisation, in which case it can be fixed with adhesives, stitchery or by other means.

Children should be introduced to the various qualities of adhesives, and given practice in handling them appropriately.

Encouraging children to use one shape on another; to see the possibilities of overlapping and overlaying; to be aware of the potential of colour, and textural contrasts and subtleties, lays the foundations on which later art experience can be built.

As children develop, they can be introduced to aspects of symmetry and informal balance, and to awareness of positive and negative shapes. Problems of creating mood, feeling, movement and areas of interest can be considered. Some subjects from stories, poems or songs lend themselves to a textural interpretation. Birds, fish, reptiles and other animals and insects are all appropriate. Bark and foliage, aerial views of landscape or townscape all offer many possibilities for experimenting with pattern and texture. It is of the greatest importance that children should carry out their own ideas. Teacher-drawn shapes should have no place in a classroom where children are learning to come to terms with problems for themselves. The value of collage experience is that children learn to select and manipulate materials in order to fulfil a purpose. Directed and unthinking use of techniques is both a sadly-missed opportunity and a waste of valuable materials.

Using collage as a 'drawing experience' or a means of analysis in looking at natural objects and environmental studies is of great value. The study of a stuffed owl, for example, might involve looking, matching and analytic skills. Drawing by cutting and tearing pieces from the resource box introduces interesting problems of matching shape, colour and texture. Clearly, some 'subjects' lend themselves to a textural response more than others. Embellishment in the use of print, paint, drawing, or stitchery can enrich the experience.

Discussion is an integral part of the experience; visual and tactile qualities of colour, mass, line and shape, contrast and effects; roughness, smoothness, shiny and matt surface, should prove an interesting beginning. When seen in this context, collage is a valuable learning experience in its own right; the end product – if there is one – is but the tip of the iceberg.

'There was an Old Man with a Beard: (Edward Lear)'. Girl. 6 years. Pencil, paint and collage. 380 × 250 mms.

'My Cat'. Girl. 7 years. Collage and chalk drawing. 250 × 375 mms.

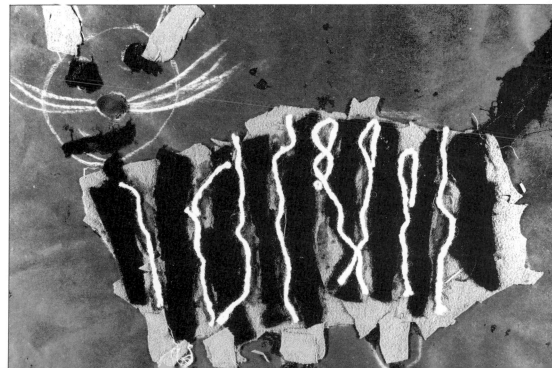

Study of an onion section using wool, thread and fibres. 11 years.

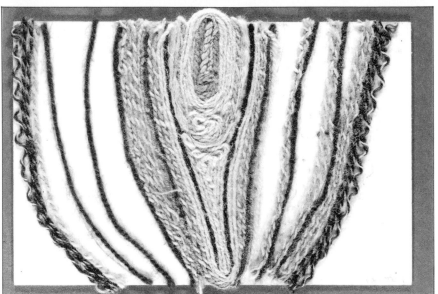

TEXTILES
weaving, appliqué, collage, stitchery, threads and fibres

What has already been outlined in the section on *Collage* is equally relevant to textiles and there is considerable overlap between the two disciplines. Early play involving handling threads, cottons, wools, raffia, linen, grass, reed, manmade fibres and fabrics of all kinds (even if only in very small pieces) will introduce children to the qualities of materials. Pulling apart cloth and threads builds up knowledge of how they were made; sorting and selecting activities in colour, texture and shape, leading to sticking, stapling, sewing or tying in swatches, will introduce discrimination.

Construction and weaving can begin with very young children (of 3 or 4), using simple frame or stiff card looms with strong wool or string warps. A strip warp using two parallel legs of a chair is also useful, and the chair can continue its normal function when not being 'woven' – provided the work is firmly attached! Hoops, bicycle and other wheel rims offer alternative shapes. The 'bit box' should include a random selection of items as children enjoy selecting and using some surprising things.

With experience, appropriate guidance and encouragement, greater discrimination and skill become apparent. Teachers should not under-estimate the high degree of craftsmanship some six year olds can reach.

Challenges can be introduced in many forms. Selections of colour, qualities of texture, contrasts, colours evocative of the elements or seasons can prove fruitful. As the child reaches the stage of matching colours, analysis of skies, colours from a stone, shell, bird, animal, or even a painting or item might be used.

A large scale weaving for group work can be set up using structures already in the school – framing of any kind, stairways and bannisters, wrought iron, 'Dexion' or other display structures, racks etc. These, of course, may have to be seen as temporary artefacts!

Using threads and fibres in a variety of ways will extend the child's knowledge of the nature of the materials, and their potential. This will be a valuable contribution to later experience in art, design and home economics disciplines. Pleating, pinning, stapling, sticking and sewing can all evolve, developing creative and problem solving skills.

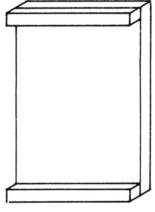

Example of a Weaving Frame

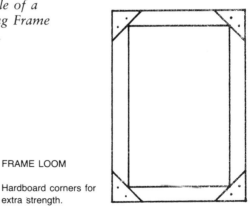

1 Square section wood, approx 1″ × 1″ nailed from back. Offcut of chipboard or plywood. Minimum ⅜″.

2 FRAME LOOM

Hardboard corners for extra strength.

Cutting As soon as they are able to handle them, children should be introduced to scissors and taught how to use them. It is very important that appropriate tools are used, and that they are suitable for the job. Provided that the child is encouraged to respect and take care in handling them, sharp scissors cause fewer accidents than blunt ones – although, of course, very sharp pointed scissors are dangerous. Games involving the cutting up of threads, paper and fabrics from the bit box into small pieces for use in collage are useful and fun. 'Drawing' freely by cutting paper or fabric shapes is also useful for building up ideas and skills.

Stitchery should be introduced as soon as the child is able to handle a needle. Teachers should experiment with the kinds of needle, thread and materials they offer the children, as it would appear that there are times when very young children are given tools and materials which are almost impossible to use!

As with cutting, the use of the needle should be taught, but the actual stitchery may well be livelier if it is based on experimental patterning, or used as a 'drawing' medium. Specific stitches may well be introduced as the child gains dexterity and skill; again, children should be encouraged to be inventive in using these in a number of ways and for different purposes. It is interesting to consider, for example, the possibilities of straight stitches, which can be built up into fabulous designs (as is apparent in Chinese embroidery or tapestry and canvas work of all kinds). The poverty of some approaches to 'binca' work, with limited design challenges, poor colour, and low expectation of stitchery experience, demonstrate a good opportunity missed. Such material can be used as a basis for rich constructions of colour, texture, patterns and pictures.

Soft sculpture, where children are encouraged to cut patterns and join and embellish components, is an excellent basis for construction in pliable materials and fabrics. It also introduces pattern cutting and stitchery to the upper junior age range.

It is well within the ability of many children to design shapes (perhaps initially in newspaper). These might be of geometric forms, fish, birds, animals or other items from the natural environment, in two (or later more) sections. These shapes can be decorated and embellished by sticking and stitchery before joining the parts. Original soft toy making can also be introduced in this way. The introduction of other materials, for example, wood, wire or junk items, may broaden the range of possibilities. Functional needs for 'Home corner' curtains, cushions and other items can be considered, providing the materials used are genuinely suitable for the purpose. Embellishment of other kinds of design – tie and dye or printmaking, for example, may be incorporated.

Applique and stitchery can follow on directly from collage and with experience new skills can be introduced. Some applique and sewing skills are very time-consuming, and rather than limiting young children to small, oversimplified products it is useful to consider challenges which could make use of stitched and stuck components. This enables teaching of the required skills in the context of a more exciting design.

Children's ideas about textiles will depend on the attitude of the teacher, and on what they have had experience of seeing. Both boys and girls find them interesting and rewarding. We owe it to the children to make them aware of the abundance of splendid artefacts, both functional and decorative, the world has to offer. Personal collections and items, loan schemes, museum sources – all offer first-hand experience. Pictures and slides can enhance understanding and pleasure. (Embroidery, weaving, rugs, toys and garments from all ages and cultures are appropriate.)

Textiles 1

Experimental weaving. Boy. 6 years. Bit box materials on a card loom (string warp).

Textiles 2

Weaving. (Wools on a string warp). Two girls. 8 years.

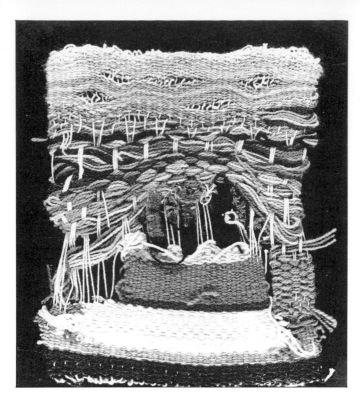

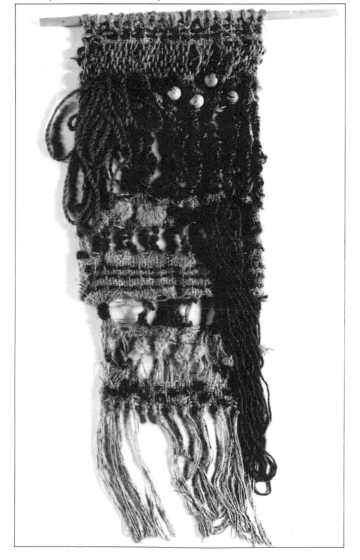

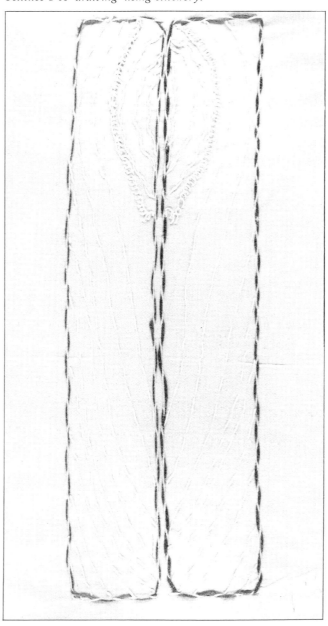

Textiles 3 Weaving on a simple frame loom.

Textiles 4 Woven textiles built on to partly 'destroyed' hessian. 10–11 years.

Textiles 5 A 'drawing' using stitchery.

*Possible developments of fabric
in the first years
Is it art? Home economics?
Science? History? Geography?
Mathematics? Language?*

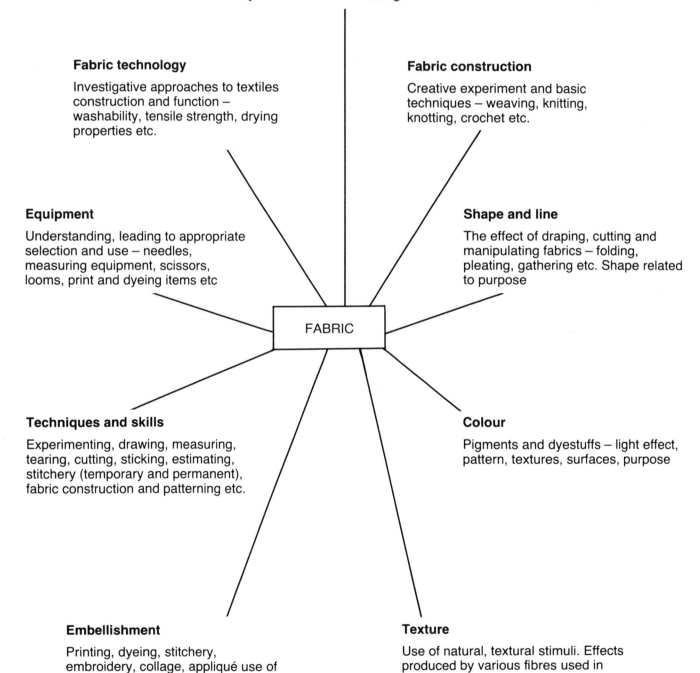

Historical aspects

Background – wool, silk, cotton,
manmade textiles. Development of
trade routes. Costume as an indicator
of ways of life and social change

Fabric technology

Investigative approaches to textiles
construction and function –
washability, tensile strength, drying
properties etc.

Fabric construction

Creative experiment and basic
techniques – weaving, knitting,
knotting, crochet etc.

Equipment

Understanding, leading to appropriate
selection and use – needles,
measuring equipment, scissors,
looms, print and dyeing items etc

Shape and line

The effect of draping, cutting and
manipulating fabrics – folding,
pleating, gathering etc. Shape related
to purpose

FABRIC

Techniques and skills

Experimenting, drawing, measuring,
tearing, cutting, sticking, estimating,
stitchery (temporary and permanent),
fabric construction and patterning etc.

Colour

Pigments and dyestuffs – light effect,
pattern, textures, surfaces, purpose

Embellishment

Printing, dyeing, stitchery,
embroidery, collage, appliqué use of
found items; purpose

Texture

Use of natural, textural stimuli. Effects
produced by various fibres used in
different ways.

> **THREE-DIMENSIONAL WORK**
> Plastic materials – clay, dough, plasticine, papier maché etc
> Rigid materials – solid forms for carving and rasping: soap, chalk, soft stone, wood, plaster etc.
> – constructional materials: card, wood, metal, plastics, wire, rolled newspaper etc
> Play, drama, textile construction – doll making, puppetry, play with environments, dressing-up, costumes etc

Three-dimensional work should be seen in balance with, and of equal importance to, two-dimensional approaches. Yet sadly, as Her Majesty's Inspectorate found in their 1978 Primary Survey, this is seldom the case.

There is a strange preconception in many branches of education that two-dimensional work is a necessary precursor to modelling, building and working; on consideration, the opposite is more logical for many children and adults. The foundation for knowledge and learning is laid on direct experience of our very three-dimensional world. Buildings, furniture, household effects, vehicles, toys, machines, seeds, plants, trees, shells, pebbles, animals – and we ourselves – are all three-dimensional phenomena. In human history, it is likely that ancient figurines moulded from clay were earlier creations than painted forms. If three-dimensional experience in a school is found to be lightweight, reasons should be sought and explored. Perhaps preconceptions about its relative importance, based on our own education and training, or the school tradition, may have something to do with it. Some teachers may feel inadequate about working at levels deeper than the superficial manipulation of plastic materials or so-called 'junk' construction – often only too aptly named!

It may be felt that sophisticated equipment is essential (kilns, pugmills and wheels, for instance) and that technical problems and messy procedures are too much for the teacher and classroom to cope with. While recognising such fears, we believe that they can be overcome and that three-dimensional work should be seen for what it is – a basic mode of experience and learning, and one which can lead to the deeper understanding and development of two-dimensional concepts.

Plastic materials – dough, plasticine, clay etc. Children need to handle and experience materials of many kinds. For very young children, sand and water play offers an early initiation, and skills can be further developed through the use of dough. Plasticine offers interesting possibilities for modelling and imprinting, but there is nothing quite like clay, with its unique 'feel' and malleable qualities. Clay has been used by man from time immemorial; it can take an immense variety of forms, ranging from the simplest squeezings and imprints to sophisticated and complex models and pottery.

The results of children's experiments with clay can simply be left to harden until interest wanes, then broken down and reconstituted. Alternatively, the work can be made permanent by firing, and decorated with ceramic colours and glazes.

It is important at all stages to surround children with interesting stimuli, in order to enhance their awareness of form and shape. A variety of pebbles, shells, fir cones, seed heads, eggs, fruit and other natural and manmade forms should play a major role in classroom displays, 'feely' boxes and bags. All clay activities are concerned with 'feel' and touch, together with visual awareness and the exploration of form, space and texture. They are related to the sensory motor phase of operations, in which the children become aware of qualities – initially through using their hands, and later with the introduction of tools.

Most children enjoy handling lumps of malleable clay (which should be soft, but not sticky). Large pieces encourage them to use both hands; basing the clay on the work surface, they will push and pull, squeeze, make holes, break pieces off and rejoin them. Smaller, hand-sized lumps encourage them to develop an awareness of shape and form in the round.

The most useful way to describe this sort of activity is *Claywork*. The term 'pottery' may lead children to expect that they will be making pots, rather than responding to the material in all its diverse possibilities.

Early experiment and play with clay is akin to the two-dimensional 'scribble' experience. This leads naturally to recognition – and naming – of forms and qualities. Often, a piece of clay will move through a series of subject namings before taking its final form. Items commonly produced at this stage include heads, figures, animals, birds, nests and eggs, houses, cars, pots and containers of various forms and functions, together with more amorphous shapes.

Experience and discussion of natural and manmade stimuli is crucial if the children's awareness of form and feel, texture, pattern, weight and temperature qualities is to develop. Challenges to build 'pebble' shapes can be interesting in their own right, or the ideas can be developed into birds, animals and abstract shapes by pulling out extensions and projections. Models and pots can be based on shell, plant or seed forms, suggesting new ways of 'seeing'.

The experience of handling clay can be extended in many ways. Squeezing shapes, patting or rolling with the hands, tapping them on the table, pinching pieces to see how thin they can be made . . . all help build up skills and stimulate fresh ideas. Comparison and discussion can further enhance the exploration.

Clay modelling can develop quite naturally into a kind of three-dimensional drawing, given appropriate encouragement. The teacher should aim to involve the children by selecting interesting stimuli, 'talking them round' the form, and encouraging them to look at, touch and feel the item. The guinea pig project on page 149 is a good example of this way of working.

This sort of support is particularly important if children have had a limited or rigid 'linear drawing' experience of art, and display some resistance to working with clay. Where children do not have sufficient background experience to make appropriate value judgements on this kind of work, they should be given many opportunities to look at models and forms, past and present.

Impetus and interest will build up as children gain confidence and experience. Self-generated ideas will develop alongside challenges suggested by the teacher. Techniques such as pinching, coiling, slabbing, joining, decorating, sgraffito etc. can be introduced with children of seven or eight, but always in the context of the ideas or design, rather than as arid skills. Children who have been taught these techniques *per se* sometimes see the skill as a 'one off' experience rather than as a 'language' to use in different ways – they may inform a new teacher that they have already 'done' coil pots!

In time, children should be provided with a rich diet of modelling and relief work, using hands and tools. The context must always be that of enabling personal discovery, expression and ways of working, rather than the isolation of 'end products'. Human beings have made ceramic forms for nearly as long as their history is known – and they continue to do so. This enables us to introduce children to examples from the past as well as from the present day. Visits to museums, items brought into school, books and illustrations, all offer varied experience of functional, fine art and design forms.

Firing If the school has a kiln it may be possible to fire some of the items and add glazes, but the experience of working with clay is worthwhile even if this is not possible.

Sawdust kilns are a simple expedient which can offer great excitement (see Figure 4.1). These kilns smoulder rather than flame, and can take up to 24–36 hours to burn through. The pots will be a mixture of greys and blacks when fired, and therefore rely on form, texture or burnishing for visual interest.

When firing it is important that the work is completely dried out and that the clay is clear of air pockets. Items over a certain thickness (1–4cm, depending on the kind of clay) should be hollow, and either constructed in that way, or scooped out with a wire loop or other suitable tool. For long, narrow forms the introduction of a pointed dowelling rod or pencil should suffice.

"Horse and Foal". Girl. 10 years.
Ceramic 140 × 70 mms.

Figure 4.1 Simple sawdust kiln

(a)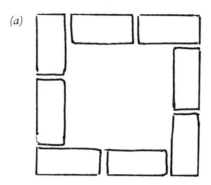

(b)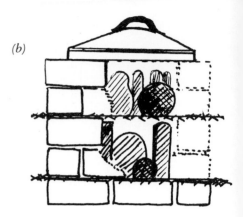

Breakages during firing should be examined and discussed in order to find reasons for the difficulties – rather than hiding items for fear of disappointment.

1 Lay bricks (**a**)
2 Lay wire mesh sheet across bricks to support pots (**b**)
3 Build up bricks to the height of pots
4 Fill with sawdust
5 Place wire mesh sheet across bricks to support second layer of pots
6 Build up bricks to height of pots
7 Fill with sawdust
8 Make long spills of newspaper and embed them in the top of the sawdust. Light
9 Place galvanized lid on top
(This kiln could be built up to three or more sections if required.)
Allow to cool completely before dismantling.

Note The kiln should be placed away from buildings, and in a protected place where children will not come into contact with it.

The outside of the kiln does not in fact get dangerously hot, but the lid could cause a minor burn if it were touched in the early part of the firing.

Basic equipment, tools and materials for clay work

Hands Children should be encouraged to use their hands in moulding, modelling and imprinting with clay prior to the introduction of any tools.

Modelling tools will in the main, or entirely, be made up of found and improvised items – blunt knives; spoon handles; clothes pegs; lolly sticks; large nails and screws; wire; buttons; plastic, metal and wooden items of all kinds; natural forms including wood, shells, fir cones, stones etc. This range can be extended by the purchase of a few wood, plastic and wire modelling tools.

Clay cutter A length of nylon or fine wire attached at either end to small pieces of dowelling rod or cotton reels is very effective.

Bow cutter for cutting slabs.

Rolling pins or pieces of broom handle can be used for slabbing and tile making. (Two wooden lathes of appropriate thickness placed flat on either side of the clay and rolled across ensure that the slab is even.)

Plastic sheeting (heavy duty) can be used for covering desk tops and floor areas.

Polythene/plastic bags are needed to store clay and to keep work damp.

Boards Wood, hardwood, linoleum tiles etc are useful to use as work bases and can vary in size.

Banding wheels or turntables allow children to look at their work from different angles.

Clay

Clay The kind of clay chosen will depend very much on the kind of work undertaken and the teacher's personal preference. Perhaps the most important aspect is to see that it is in the right condition – not too sticky, not too dry. Readily available clay bodies range from smooth 'red' and 'buff' suitable for fine work to the more open textured 'crank mixture' suitable for thicker work. Oxidising St Thomas' Body is an excellent all round clay if only one is used. It can be fired from 1000°C to 1280°C. It is sufficiently open to enable thicker work, or it can be modelled quite finely if so desired.

To reconstitute clay Partially dry clay may be put into a strong, unperforated plastic bag with water, tied well and trampled or worked from the outside until a good consistency is achieved. It can also be damped down in bins and worked thoroughly. Completely dry clay should be soaked and mixed. The resulting slurry can be laid out on wooden boards or plaster slabs to dry to the appropriate consistency.

Slips These consist of creamy mixtures of clay and water which are used for joining clay and for decoration – for example a red clay slip could be painted on a buff clay model while it is still damp. Further colours can be obtained by staining the slips with small quantities of ceramic colours. Joining clay is facilitated by using tools or old toothbrushes dipped in water before roughening the surfaces to be joined.

Clay storage Clay should be stored in airtight bins, preferably on casters for ease of movement, or used directly from polythene bags which can then be resealed.

Glazes should be fired to temperatures recommended by the manufacturers. A glaze is really glass which can be made from an infinite number of combinations of materials. The clay is usually fired once (the biscuit firing) then glazed and fired again (the glaze firing).

Plaster

Plaster may be used for casting, making moulds, modelling on an armature, or for carving and rasping. Care must be taken to keep it away from claywork which is to be fired.

Papier mâché

Papier mâché is a mixture of wet paper and a water-based adhesive (*Polycell* is excellent for this purpose). It can be pulped and modelled like clay or applied in sheets and strips over supporting surfaces and structures. Soft wire armatures, wire-mesh shapes, pebbles, plates, clay or plasticine models, polythene bottles or balloons etc are useful basic shapes to build on. Treatment of the surface of the item with soap solution or *Vaseline* allows the papier mâché form to be lifted off when dry. Figures, masks, headgear, receptacles, stage props and models of all kinds and scale can be made. The material allows for vigorous modelling, so that the end products become interesting forms in their own right, rather than pale shadows of the underlying shapes.

Construction and modelling (Junk?)

A collection of waste products and containers of all kinds can form the basis of fruitful art and design work. The nature and quality of the materials available will govern the value of the work. Consideration of size should encompass items to construct environments, towers and other 'maxi' pieces, and, at the other end of the scale, 'miniature' pieces.

Building coil pots using a mould as a base.

Moulded dishes.
Environmental Stimuli.
11 years.

The *'maxi' experience* – crates, big boxes, tubes, wood, bricks, cardboard, sheeting, rope, tins, corrugated card, polystyrene pieces etc.

The *'mini' experience* – tiny boxes, tins, containers, matchsticks, lolly sticks, wood, small pieces of fabric, plastic, metal etc.

Carving

It is possible for children to enjoy a sculptural experience in discovering forms by taking away part of the 'block' by means of cutting, carving, rasping or filing. Suitable materials include soap, newly-cast plaster blocks, firm clay, wood, polystyrene etc. Safety must always be considered, and vices for holding the blocks will be necessary. Pupils must be taught to handle tools (appropriate to their ability) safely. *Surforms* are excellent tools for rasping, and can be obtained in a variety of shapes.

Mealtime. 11 years.
Ceramic. (Table
100 mms., square)

Studies of a Skate egg. 10–11 years.
Drawings, pattern cutting, making into a stuffed fabric form, modelling, glazing and firing in clay.

PUPPETRY

Puppetry can be a very exciting area of experience. Helen Binyon suggests that its essence lives in movement and that it is a 'form of communication between performers and audience'. She goes on to say that the 'work of art is not the puppet but the performance'.

This potential for communication between child and child; child and adult; child and audience; may be fulfilled in many ways, using different techniques. Puppetry can be based on pure movement, colour and form, or it can involve rhythm, music and words. There is much to learn about puppets throughout the world, past and present. Puppets are a valuable historical and ethnic resource, as well as offering the possibility of basing challenges on historical stimuli and folklore.

There are four traditional types of puppet – *hand, rod, string* (marionette) and *shadow*.

It is very important for children to be able to experiment before building puppets for a purpose. Quick (5 minute) constructions on the hand, arm or stick can be used in spontaneous movement, possibly with the addition of rhythms or words (between two puppets, or using a mirror). A rich bit box is a necessity – constantly replenished with interesting papers, fabrics, foils, plastics and natural materials – together with items suitable for heads: bags, old tennis and table-tennis balls, tights, stockings, socks, boxes, fibre plant pots, plastic bottles etc.

Scale can vary considerably, from finger puppets to very large rod puppets. Glove and rod puppets offer a variety of possibilities, involving problem solving as the design evolves and develops, and developing skills of selection, sewing, sticking, pinning, painting and organising.

Hand or glove puppetry is a self-explanatory term, but it often evokes an image limited to the sterile 'mitten topped by a grotesque head' so popular in the 'how to do it' manuals. In fact, if glove puppets are based on the adornment of the hand, hands or arms, possibly with extensions built on to the fingers by means of buckram or paper tubes, for example, they offer much more potential.

Simple hand puppets can be very immediate and personal to the child. They sometimes prove useful in building up confidence, when used as a device to speak through.

Rod puppets are quite different in character and can be built in decorative, elegant, fantastic or grotesque forms. Traditionally, they are found in China, Thailand, India, Africa and Java. In human and animal puppets the central rod runs through the body and is fixed firmly in the head, enabling it to be rotated. Arms or extensions are moved by means of rods or wires. Robes can be rich and full, and often play a significant part in movement and sound.

Hand and rod puppets are worked from below and it is therefore necessary to construct some kind of screening for the animators, which will also allow for scenery and props. (The tradition of the small acting area stemmed originally from the Punch and Judy man's need to mask the mysteries of his show.) A useful classroom solution is to construct a screen of appropriate height along the length of a classroom wall in front of a pinboard surface, allowing space for a number of children. The back cloth can be mounted on the pinboard and other props attached to the screen itself. Different scenes can be set up along the length of the screen, as a backing for journeys and chases.

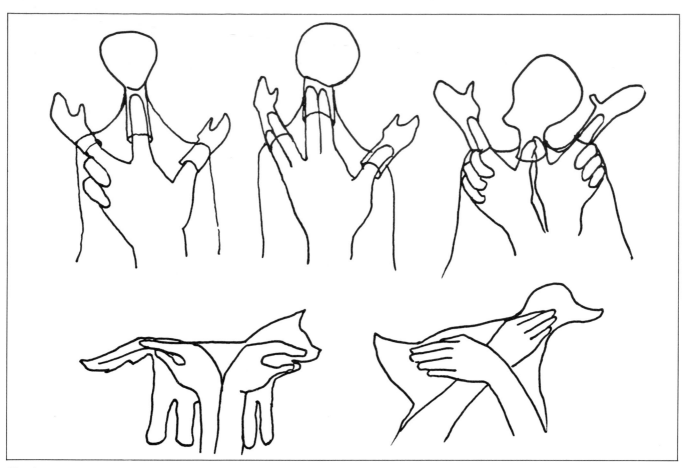

Hand puppets

Rod puppets.
Wires and rod supports.

Rod puppets. 9 years.

String puppets (Marionettes) are less usual in the early years, but it is possible for children who are highly motivated and who have the appropriate abilities, to use them. These puppets are moved by means of strings from above, by hands, or on a pattern of wooden struts constructed to enable specific movements.

Shadow puppets have their roots in Chinese, Indonesian, Indian, Egyptian and Turkish origins. They are essentially two-dimensional. Basic necessities are a screen of translucent material and a light source behind it. Moving objects/puppets are held between the two. A suitable screen can be easily constructed by stretching smooth, cotton-type material tightly over a wooden frame. Scenery can be pushed into the side of the screen frame, or attached to the fabric by means of sellotape.

The rods which enable the puppets to move are fixed in either horizonatal or vertical positions – the mode of lighting will depend on the type chosen. Horizontal

Fig. 4.2 Shadow puppet. Strip light and screen.

dowelling rods, fixed firmly to the puppet by means of drawing pins and glue, will require a strip light placed a little way back from the screen (30–40cm, 12–18in) and level with the base (Figure 4.2).

Vertical rods and wires can be firmly fixed to the puppet, which is then illuminated by a projector set up behind the animators and above their heads (unless they are to be part of the show). Using this method, changes of scale can be achieved by shifting the puppet between the screen and light source, and many variations using objects, slides and gels are possible.

The puppets can be made from sheet material, card, paper etc. The children can experiment by holding items between the light source and the screen and by cutting out a figure (possible already drawn or painted) from news- or sugar paper. For horizontal rod puppets one rod fixed firmly to the figure by means of a drawing pin will allow a surprising amount of animation when rotated and moved, and it is generally only a short time before the children have the idea of making moving parts by cutting and rejoining or designing. Joints should move freely – thread knotted on either side of the joined parts allows greater flexibility (some children will need help with this process). Much discussion and problem solving can take place with developments in the design: trial runs using newspaper and scrap; experiment with different positioning of the rods; consideration of the number of rods desirable and possible . . . Shapes and patterns can be cut from the figure to add interest and transparent colour (tissue, gel, cellophane etc) appended or used as infills. Shadow puppets can evolve into every possible shape and form – human, bird, fish, animal, plants, clouds, houses, geometric and amorphous shapes.

Children will develop many interesting ideas of their own, but the opportunity to look at historical examples of two-dimensional work can be of interest. Challenges to build plays and stories around Greek pottery decoration, Egyptian painting, North American Indian painting and beadwork, or the Bayeux Tapestry, will require some real research and involve the translation of one design form into another.

Doll-making, allied to puppetry, is of interest to both boys and girls. Motivation may come from available materials, or from research into costume. Simple or sophisticated dolls can be constructed from stockings, rags, bottles or cartons, to suit the children's practical or planned design.

Response to Artefacts

Many teachers go to endless trouble to find illustrations they deem suitable for children, yet fail to see the rich vein of experience offered through the art and design forms surrounding us. The purpose of introducing children to this experience is twofold: first as a means of inspiring interest and enjoyment in our own heritage and those of other cultures; second in order to extend the range of the child's expectation with regard to art and design. Children are bombarded by imagery through the media, advertisements and various graphic forms; they deserve to be introduced to other qualities and values.

There is no real substitute for first-hand experience. Excursions to galleries and museums, visits by artists and craftsmen, and seeing original work brought into school are the best kind of introduction. The idea that looking at works of art calls for a sophisticated 'History of Art' response is mistaken. Artists and craftsmen were – and are – direct creators working to their own ideas or at the behest of others. Art History, although a valid discipline in its own right, has little to do with this process.

Original works have their own energy, vitality and surface quality which no reproduction can imitate, although reproductions can offer experience of imagery and design and are therefore a useful resource. Classroom collections can be built up from cuttings, cards and books and the school library should offer a wide range of good quality reproductions of artists' and designers' work. Children's story books are often beautifully illustrated and careful selection will enable children to see many different approaches to drawing, painting, print and collage etc.

It is a mistake for teachers to prejudge what children will respond to, or only to offer pictures they consider will be popular. The object of the exercise is to allow children to think, feel, respond and discriminate in their own way and at their own level. Young children often show a direct insight into works which adults consider too sophisticated for them, and respond to aesthetic qualities of colour, mood, form or shape as readily as to subject matter.

It is necessary for teachers, in the first stages of planning this aspect of the art experience, to look carefully at their own expectations regarding children's responses and to be willing to experiment in order to gain some insight. The following case study illustrates this point.

An experiment was devised by which teachers could *a)* see how individual children and later, groups, responded to a variety of images; and *b)* study the children's responses and gain insight into the way in which they were thinking, understanding and using language and vocabulary. The 'test' was simple. Sets of ten colour reproductions of diverse subject matter, ranging from abstract to realist,

Discussion and practical work using originals and reproductions.

ancient to modern, but all approximately the same size, were numbered and mounted. A questionnaire was evolved and individual children were invited to look at a set of reproductions during breaks or lunch hours. (The timing precluded children being influenced by their peers.)

The teachers drew up the following guidelines for using the questionnaire:

CHILDREN'S RESPONSE TO PAINTINGS

The words 'PICTURE' or 'PATTERN' should *NOT* be used.

METHOD	Spread the 10 pictures on a surface where they can all easily be seen.
INTRODUCTION	'I WANT YOU TO LOOK VERY CAREFULLY AT THESE'

(work through questions 1–5 gently and conversationally but without discussion.

Question 1	Which one do you like best?
Question 2	Which one do you like second best?
Question 3	Which one do you like third best?
Question 4	Which one do you think I like best?
Question 5a	Are there any you do not like?
b	(spaces for other numbers if more than one disliked)
c	(spaces for other numbers if more than one disliked)

Having completed questions 1–5 ask each child why he/she chose answers to Question 1 (best), Question 4 (which one you would like best), Question 5 (which one not liked).

Finally allow free discussion, influencing as little as possible.

In working with individuals, the teacher was at pains not to influence the child's response in any way and merely accepted what was said, pleasantly, refraining from making remarks of any kind at the beginning of the 'session'.

Initially, the child was invited to 'look at these pictures' and then asked which ones he liked best. It came to light after a number of teachers had put this into practice, that children were not choosing abstract works or patterns because they thought they had to choose 'a picture'! The first question was therefore modified to 'look at *these*'. The teacher noted, without discussion, which three works the child liked best and which he did not like; also which picture the child thought the teacher would like best.

Following this exchange a discussion ensued, with the teachers doing their best not to influence or lead the child. Some teachers tape-recorded these sessions, and were more than a little amused, and horrified, at realising how much they were, in spite of themselves, letting slip their own prejudices and value judgements.

The children's answers as to the artform which they felt their teacher liked best proved enlightening. In many cases the children had picked up clues from what the teacher wore, selected in other contexts, or said when talking about children's art. One class had all, individually, chosen a Mexican mural as the teacher's favourite work. It was flat, hard-edged and hard coloured, a little like the interlocking shapes of a jigsaw puzzle, with stylised figures and complicated background. The teacher hated it and could not understand the unanimity of her class on the subject. Her colleagues discussed it with her and on being pressed as to what she said to children when they were working, after initially saying that she did not say anything much, she admitted to a few comments she made on occasions. These included 'bright colours', 'mind the edges' and 'fill in the background'!

Figure 4.3 shows the form devised by the teachers to gauge children's response to artefacts (Suffolk Education Authority).

Figure 4.4 is an example of the form with the children's responses filled in.

Figure 4.3

Suffolk Education Committee

CHILDREN'S RESPONSE TO ARTEFACTS   Date ....

School ....

Artists and Titles of Work

1		6	
2		7	
3		8	
4		9	
5		10	

AGE	NAME	Q1	Q2	Q3	Q4	Q5a	b	c		COMMENTS
									Q1	
									Q5	
									Q1	
									Q5	
									Q1	
									Q5	
									Q1	
									Q5	
									Q1	
									Q5	
									Q1	
									Q5	
									Q1	
									Q5	

GENERAL COMMENTS

* This page may be reproduced for use in schools.

Figure 4.4

CHILDREN'S RESPONSE TO ARTEFACTS   Date ...*October 1984*...........................

School ...*Town Primary*.........................

Artists and Titles of Work

1	Matisse. Flowers + Pottery.	6	Picasso. Woman in a chemise (blue period)
2	Sassetta. Journey of the Magi	7	El Greco. St Jerome as Cardinal.
3	Monet. Regatta at Argenteuil	8	Rembrandt. Self portrait.
4	Durer. Virgin and child.	9	Uccello. Battle of San Romano
5	Hockney. Swimming pool.	10	Masson. Iroquois Landscape. (abstract)

AGE	NAME	Q1	Q2	Q3	Q4	Q5a	b	c		COMMENTS
7	Tracy.	4. Durer	2. Sassetta	5. Monet	1. Matisse	8. Rembrandt	7. El Greco		Q1	Its a mother and baby. She is wearing lovely clothes. It is a lovely garden.
									Q5	He hasn't kept to the edges.
8	Maria.	10. Masson	5. Hockney	3. Monet	1. Matisse	9. Uccello	7. El Greco		Q1	The colours look nice together. They are lovely swirly shapes.
									Q5	They are fighting. I don't like those people.
8	Paula.	2. Sassetta	3. Monet	4. Durer	10. Masson	8. Rembrandt	6. Picasso		Q1	There are lots of people and horses and things, and birds in the sky. I know where they are going.
									Q5	Its all blurry, and theres nothing in the background.
8	Scott	10. Masson	1. Matisse	3. Sassetta	1. Matisse	7. El Greco	8. Rembrandt	6. Picasso	Q1	I can see lots of things in the shapes. Those colours are all warm.
									Q5	Its all dirty.
8	Jonathon	3. Monet	5. Hockney	3. Sassetta	1. Matisse	6. Picasso	7. El Greco		Q1	Because I like boats, and it's a nice day.
									Q5	Its all one colour, and its bare.
9	Martin.	8. Rembrandt.	6. Picasso	3. Monet	3. Monet	9. Uccello			Q1	I like this one. The man is all sad. He hasn't got anywhere to live.
									Q5	Its false. — too tidy.
8	Richard.	1. Matisse	3. Monet	4. Durer	10. Masson	6. Picasso			Q1	Lovely colours. The blue is special. There are lots of round shapes.
									Q5	Its not finished is it?

GENERAL COMMENTS The children were interested, and clearly showed their preconceptions. How many of these have I built up? The children's choice of my favourite picture was arrived at, it seems, by my encouraging them to paint boldly, and to mix strong interesting colours. One child knew of my interest in sailing. In fact Monet would have been my choice.
One child (not listed) chose the El Greco portrait as he thought it was 'God writing in the Bible'! None of the others interested him.

From initial considerations three approaches evolved:

1 ENCOURAGING CHILDREN TO LOOK AT AND RESPOND NATURALLY TO ART AND DESIGN FORMS

In this approach the experience is paramount and there is no overt follow up unless the child initiates it.

2 ENCOURAGING CHILDREN TO IMMERSE THEMSELVES DEEPLY IN EXPERIENCING ART FORMS AND TALKING ABOUT THEIR RESPONSES

Possible questions might be:

What do you think this artist is trying to show us? Tell us . . ?
What is this about? How can you tell . . ?
What can you find out by looking at this . . ?
What story does this picture tell . . ?
What does this make you feel? Why . . ?
What kind of colours have been used . . ?
What kind of person do you think this is? Why do you say that . . ?
Are these 'real life' colours? If not – why not . . ?
Does this remind you of anything . . ?

Examples

Two block-mounted reproductions were introduced – a De Vlaminck 'Storm' and a Constable landscape. Subject matter was discussed and described and the best distance for viewing considered. This proved to be a revelation for some children, as they had never thought about this aspect before. It also gave them insight into looking at their own and their peers' work. The Constable picture was considered 'best' when the question of which work appeared the most real was raised, but the De Vlaminck was adjudged better when the kind of weather was discussed.

The children chose a reproduction (from 10 displayed) and were asked to respond to the way it made them feel. A number chose Romney's *Laughing Girl* – a very dark painting with the top half of the girl (very white) leaning her head on her bare arms. The title was indistinct and all of the children said it was a sad picture, adding comments – 'She's been locked in her room' or 'Like someone has left home.' They were clearly responding to the range of colour and tone and showed surprise when one of them deciphered the title. One child said Rossetti's *Beata Beatrice* was a happy picture – 'Because it was like Summer'. Asked why, he replied, 'Because the bird is bringing her flowers' . . . 'What is she doing? . . . 'Praying, I think' . . . 'Could she be dreaming?' . . . 'No' (pointing to the figures in the background) 'Because its all happening.'
Turner's *Fighting Temeraire* was enjoyed by many children, and the time of day and colours were discussed. The feelings were 'sad' – Why? – 'Because I think it is a ghost ship and the little black boat in front looks all strong . . .' Other developments included the selection of a series of artforms on the same subject matter – for example human heads, trees, animals, buildings, landscapes or abstracts. Selections of illustrations from children's books were also considered.

3 ENCOURAGING PRACTICAL WORK IN RELATION TO ARTEFACTS

A number of aspects can be subsumed under this heading including children responding through practical work to artefacts taken into the school or seen elsewhere or by consideration of practical problems artists have dealt with (colour, atmosphere, brushwork, form, mixing and matching colours, pattern and texture, for example).

Some examples of developments in practical work

One group of six-year-old children selected their 'picture for the week' from a group and discussed it for a few moments each day. The subject matter was a Monet landscape with windmill. When it had been returned to the loan scheme a child said 'I wish I could paint pictures like the picture we had on the wall'. The teacher said 'I'm sure you could', but was surprised when the child, joined by three friends, went off to do that very thing. The result (which was from memory) was interesting. All the children had remembered the subject matter and general proportions of the picture.

The placement of the windmill and other shapes in the composition was surprisingly accurate in three pieces of work; it was centrally placed by one child. The colour was scumbled and broken and in the appropriate colour range in three paintings. The fourth was flat, but was representational. All these children, in their own work, were still at the symbolist stage, and used a line of blue for the sky and a band of green for the grass in a typical symbolist manner. In these paintings in all four children's work, the whole picture area was covered, as in the original painting.

David Downes, a Suffolk schoolboy, whose work was exhibited in developmental sequence in the *Six Children Draw* Exhibition, (London University Institute of Education and Suffolk Education Authority 1982), was profoundly influenced by seeing reproductions of works of art when he was eight years old.

> He (David) found a reproduction of a painting by Constable in his calendar collection and pressed his parents to find more – 'I like Constable pictures so much' he says 'because they look so nice – they were drawn so nicely with paint'. David devised a game whereby the family 'sold' reproductions in exchange for cards he made himself. At least fifty of these were drawn ... some of these drawings are detailed and intricate but would take as little as ten minutes to accomplish if he were deeply involved. He began to use water colour and pastel (new to him) in order to get Constable effects, and although he did not copy the cards, a definite influence in the selection of subject matter and the manner in which he composed his pictures using colour mass is apparent.
>
> When no more Constable reproductions were available some works by Lowry were introduced and for six weeks David became very interested, with his work proliferating small houses and figures drawn whilst he sang the *Matchstick men* song popular at the time.
>
> Turner became an even greater attraction and David was enthralled by his work. In his own drawings an atmospheric quality developed through the use of clear watercolour washes and broadly used pastels with outline disappearing completely at times.
>
> *Six Children Draw* David Downes 4–11 years. Margaret Morgan

The developments in David's work were entirely self motivated. They were undertaken at home and generally encouraged by his parents but no tuition as such took place. This kind of experience gives credence to Brent and Marjorie Wilson's beliefs that 'Children learn to draw by seeing other drawings'.

NATIONAL DEVELOPMENTS

A number of major projects on this subject have been undertaken in recent years and show fascinating developments and educational potential for children of all ages and abilities. They include the following:

The Illuminating Experience, and *Broadening the Context* – Schools Council project directed by Rod Taylor of the Drumcroon Education Art Centre, Wigan. This work has led to the publication of an excellent book: *Educating for Art*.

The Real Thing – Children's use of Works of Art – Devon Education Authority project directed by Robert Clement. (This material is also included in *The Art Teachers Handbook* by R Clement, Hutchinson 1987)

Using Pictures with Children John Bowden, Art Advisors' Association.

These projects, whilst showing different approaches, unanimously testify to the value of the experience. Although each of them deals with the full educational age range they are valuable acquisitions to any staff library.

The projects contain a wealth of examples of interesting practice, some of which are included in this publication. All use a strong component of discussion, challenge, sensitive questioning and listening on the part of the teacher or director, as the following extracts illustrate.

Reconstruction or simulation of work of art as basis for objective work
9/10 year olds observed and talked about 'Still Life with Goldfish' by Matisse and then made their own paintings of a similar composition which was set up for them within their classroom.

8/10 year olds observed and talked about a series of etchings of buildings, including the work of Valerie Thornton. This was followed by observation of the different views of buildings that could be seen from the school windows and playground and the children's own drawings of those buildings. In this they were clearly influenced by the different viewpoints of buildings seen in the original works studied.

Teacher's description of a painting/drawing as stimulus
11/12 year old children. The teacher described a painting to the class but the children did not see the reproduction. The children produced their own version, based on the description. A number of variants on this particular format have been employed. With primary children the description was usually in the form of a story. Paintings with an interesting content were used, eg

Bruegel 'Hunters in the Snow' and 'Harvesters'.
Millet 'The Gleaners'
Picasso 'Les Saltimbanques'
Lautrec 'The Circus'

. . . To cope with technical problems experienced by the pupils and to encourage maximum involvement, models were posed to stimulate the effect and poses, for example, of the trudging of hunters through the snow with their spears and their 'catch' on their shoulders.
. . . Their own drawings and paintings were then compared with the picture that had been described to them. How like the original the children's works were was not of significance, but it was important that the pupils discussed varying moods, compositions, scale, sense of movement created, etc.
This comparison was important, also, in that it gave the pupils opportunity to engage in the analysis and description of each other's work while the descriptive power of the teacher's initial introduction was still fresh in their minds as a model.
This method in its initial stages has much in common with Marion Richardson's pioneering approach.

(Broadening the Context)

In making the point that observation of painting has challenged children to produce work well in advance of their normal perceptions, Robert Clement cites the example of

children who were given access to illustrations from Les Tres Riches Heures of the Duc de Berry in support of a class topic on Medieval Life produced drawings of feasts, jousting and battles that in their detail and quality were much in advance of those drawings normally produced by 8 year olds in association with this kind of theme and where the source material would consist of 20th Century versions of medieval life.

(The Real Thing)

Another example he gives is of

A class of 10 year olds who responded to the challenge to repaint a landscape by Winslow Homer and to bring about a change of mood by changing the colour balance within their version

(The Real Thing)

An example from John Bowden which offers much food for thought is the following flow diagram constructed around the painting 'Snape Landscape 1958' by P Sutton.

USING A PAINTING WITH A CLASS OF FIRST-YEAR JUNIOR PUPILS

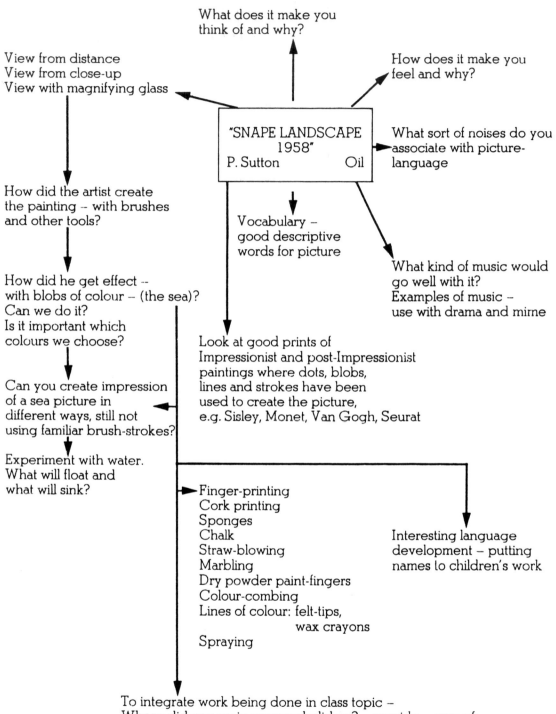

What does it make you
think of and why?

View from distance
View from close-up
View with magnifying glass

How does it make you
feel and why?

"SNAPE LANDSCAPE
1958"
P. Sutton   Oil

What sort of noises do you
associate with picture-
language

How did the artist create
the painting – with brushes
and other tools?

Vocabulary –
good descriptive
words for picture

How did he get effect –
with blobs of colour – (the sea)?
Can we do it?
Is it important which
colours we choose?

What kind of music would
go well with it?
Examples of music –
use with drama and mime

Can you create impression
of a sea picture in
different ways, still not
using familiar brush-strokes?

Look at good prints of
Impressionist and post-Impressionist
paintings where dots, blobs,
lines and strokes have been
used to create the picture,
e.g. Sisley, Monet, Van Gogh, Seurat

Experiment with water.
What will float and
what will sink?

Finger-printing
Cork printing
Sponges
Chalk
Straw-blowing
Marbling
Dry powder paint-fingers
Colour-combing
Lines of colour: felt-tips,
                    wax crayons
Spraying

Interesting language
development – putting
names to children's work

To integrate work being done in class topic –
Where did you go in summer holidays? – seaside – map of
England showing towns visited – linked with stories, poems,
writing about imaginary journey under sea – model of
undersea world – leading on to model of desert island
(and map) where Robinson Crusoe was shipwrecked.

Below, John Bowden describes a project set up by Alexandra Fairman in North Yorkshire.

One rural primary school began working with an infant class (5–7 year olds) looking at three abstract works. (Victor Vasarely, Edvardo Paolozzi and Eirran Short). The Paolozzi print was chosen to develop work in percussion.

The children constructed a code for different shapes and qualities. CIRCLES – metal instruments: SQUARES – non metal instruments: LARGE SHAPES – play slowly: DIFFERENT COLOURS were depicted as different instruments, BRIGHT COLOURS – Loudly played: PALE COLOURS – softly played.

The children enjoyed the work and developed it as far as demonstrating the sounds in isolation. Difficulties occurred in attempting to coordinate sounds into a final 'composition', and it was decided that the junior group should be instructed by the infants to undertake this next stage. This proved successful, and any fears of disappointment in 'playing the picture' were offset by the pleasure the infants showed in their role of instructors to the older children.

The whole experiment culminated into a 'performance' with the teacher beating time, or assisting by giving signs at the start and finish of each set of sounds.

The children were satisfied with the end product and the teacher felt that the children would look at abstract work in more depth, concentrating far more on subtleties of light and shade, pale and bright colours, and qualities of shape and time.

(*Using Pictures with Children*)

These examples may serve to extend our own expectation of what might be done. Every teaching situation as well as each teacher's approach will be different and appropriate experiences can be developed through art activities, conversation, drama and dressing up, movement, sound, building environments and designing etc.

The real key is the proviso that we understand that artefacts can speak to us directly, that we are in no way 'teaching taste' and that we are not holding on to too many of our preconceptions.'

Groupwork

One of the main values of groupwork is that children are challenged to work together towards a common aim. It offers opportunities for initiative, teamwork and design in action, and the 'end product' can have an impact far greater than its individual parts.

The way in which groupwork is handled can give a clear intimation as to a teacher's understanding of art and design activities – whether there is any real value and content in the work, or if a 'short-circuited window dressing' approach has been used, with teacher-planned design and drawn outlines or provision of templates and direction of techniques. It is very difficult to offer any sound educational defence for the latter approach, especially as large quantities of materials may well have been used.

Groupwork can apply to drawing, painting, collage, printmaking, dyestuffs, stitchery, fabric construction, models, relief and sculpture, or a mixture of these forms and media. If teachers appreciate that the real value lies in the skills of personal initiative and interaction, learning to plan and carry out projects and working through difficulties as they arise, they will allow for the appropriate time involvement and apparently slow build up of the work. The value is not only in the end product, but in the processes leading to it.

Ideas for subject matter are unlimited and can be built on reality, imagination or fantasy. Celebrations of the festivals – Christmas and Easter, for example – could prove to be the most valuable and exciting highlights of the year rather than the banal, expensive and time-consuming projects they sadly sometimes turn out to be!

TWO BASIC APPROACHES TO GROUPWORK

1 Unit Structures

The principle of this way of working is to consider units which can be undertaken by individual children and which will, when brought together, form a whole. These can be two- or three-dimensional in form. It is important that the children are aware from the outset of the part their 'unit' will play in the whole.

This method is especially suitable for young children as it enables them to work in a naturally egocentric way while being able to bring their offerings together in a shared piece of work. One form might be the painting/collage/dyeing of a 'setting' on to which are added various individual components. Examples of subject matter might include the following:

- 'Ourselves' in various situations – playground, party, school life, dressing up, what we would like to be, in a magic garden . . .
- Stories of giants, Gulliver, Snow Queen, dragons . . . where the characters could be shared between the group. In some cases, two children enjoy working on one figure, or unit. Decorative subjects might include undersea scenes, woodlands, birds and animals, zoos, markets, etc, changing scale to a 'worm's eye view'; or 'Tom Thumb'. Pattern units, for example, stars, snowflakes or geometrical shapes, lend themselves to printing, painting, collage and embroidery.
- Experimenting with a variety of shapes and forms in a limited range of colours, or materials, on a specific theme can offer children an excellent means of problem solving and experience, with each child offering a number of 'solutions'. For example stars could be defined in all shapes and sizes, and decorated in many different ways in one or two colours. Each child might have a small piece of silver or gold to enhance his 'unit'. These could be built up into big wall decorations, hangings, or mobiles.
- Three-dimensional 'groups' or 'scenes' could be built into cardboard cartons which could then be covered and piled into a structure.
- Models can be considered in the same way, with figures or shapes being brought together into assemblages, and scenes. 'Nativity', family groups, ships, harbours, building, etc are all appropriate and can be put into simple or complex settings and possibly lit by spotlights to add a final magic.

The children should be fully involved in discussing the placement of the units as this is an integral part of the project.

2 *Group Designs/Forms*
(Murals, friezes, sectional work, reliefs, hangings, free standing items etc)

Following the introduction or evolution of a subject or design brief, children can be challenged to work in pairs or small groups. Possibilities should be discussed and working drawings, models and notes made in profusion to form a basis for later selection. The teacher's role is to stimulate, encourage and enable problems and difficulties to be surmounted by the children. No blame should fall on those who find it difficult to work together harmoniously; the skills of handling teamwork should be seen as part of the educational process. It is a salutory experience to be one of a group of adults attempting teamwork, on occasions! Problems should be gently faced and discussed and solutions negotiated.

Individuals can be 'victimised' by a group, sometimes through no fault of their own. Where no solution appears viable, removal of the child without loss of face is important. (On one occasion the teacher invented the need for lengths of border pattern to be created to enhance a mural – which it did!) Trouble can be generated by the teacher if too many children are working on one project with too few tools or materials, and/or in a restricted space.

A SEQUENCE OF PROJECT DEVELOPMENT

1 Following the decision regarding subject matter, ideas and possible ways of working need to be discussed and lists, plans, diagrams, sketches, notes and maquettes made. (All working drafts should be kept, however scrappy to be seen as part of the working process when evaluation takes place.)

In a sensitively-guided project it is nearly always possible to find layout or plan components within the children's own ideas; it is a very poor start if the teacher takes over.

2 Next the general layout, or structural plan for the work needs to be drawn up. Very often a 'leader' or leaders will surface in the group, and these children can be invited to begin the layout based on the ideas generated by the group. Discussions regarding the required size of contents and components will prove important.

In two-dimensional work general positioning and planning can be 'roughed' in using a broad, easily erased medium (blackboard chalk is excellent for the purpose).

3 When the 'landmarks' are in place, decisions must be taken as to each child's personal responsibility. Practical problems, use of equipment and tools, organisation and any relevant restrictions must be considered.

Nativity Group. 8–11 years. Ceramic. (Standing figures 200 mms. approx.)

the giant had
enormous hands
and picked Jack
up.

Boy. 5 years. Fibre tip. 450 × 600 mms.

4 The children will need to be encouraged to stand back at intervals to consider the effects of their work and to discuss developments.
5 Finally, consideration of the finished work together with discussion as to the processes the children have been through and difficulties and successes encountered will complete the experience.

Narrative paintings/drawings/print/reliefs/textiles can all be built up by these methods. Friezes, panels showing the lives of saints, stained glass, sequences of units depicting stories, totems, cartoon strips and sequences of all shapes and sizes are all useful modes of working.

Looking at paintings, stained glass, mosaics and tapestries – Roman, Egyptian, early Christian, Indian, Chinese – can extend ideas and children readily follow the stories within the art form, or are happy to invent their own.

MATERIALS AND EQUIPMENT

Besides the normal range of materials and classroom items it is important to make sure that appropriate tools and facilities are on hand for large-scale work. Buckets and bowls will be necessary for the large quantities of paint, dye and adhesives. House painters' brushes are essential. Powder colour and tempera can be mixed with remains of emulsion paint collected from parents, for large areas.

Unit Structure. Individual units make up a large wall hanging. 1200 × 950 mms. Junior Group work.

Supports for work may include large sheets of brown paper, the flat side of corrugated card, frieze paper, canvas, hessian, cotton, hardboard, plywood and chipboard.

Note Where children lack confidence to undertake large pieces of work, games can be planned, the objective being to encourage children to work on a large scale. For example, one teacher in an infant class prepared a pile of large pieces of newspaper on the floor, prior to a story period. She mixed black powder colour into a thick, inky consistency and provided hog-hair brushes. With the children sitting around her she introduced her own story about a giant. After describing him she paused and asked if any child could paint a giant on the newspaper. A small girl complied with a fairly small giant, and the story continued. A little later, a large giant was introduced, and another child obliged with a slightly larger painting. The story continued, in fact, over three days, with larger giants appearing, and the necessity to stick pieces of paper together to hold them. All the giants were finally cut out and placed in a row along the back wall. Needless to say the experience cultivated an enthusiasm for measuring and comparing.

Photography

Photography is not an alternative to art but, in one teacher's words, 'a mixture of art, craft, design and technical know-how'. It encourages children to look and select. Children should be made aware of photographic imagery of all kinds. Most children enjoy bringing in family snaps and studies. Newspapers, books and magazines will also supplement experience and stimulate lively discussion as to the message or success of the photographs, and their technicalities.

Very young children enjoy taking snapshots and can be encouraged to look through viewfinders cut out of card, to help them choose interesting 'pictures'. (Film should be professionally developed at this stage.)

A number of schools will wish to take things further. Some have introduced photography into the curriculum or organised it as an activity or club, with the children developing and enlarging their own work. Experiments with cameras undertaken with children who have emotional learning difficulties have proved useful and constructive. The fact that a qualitative image has been produced, which the children are not ashamed to call their own, has encouraged them to continue working with a new kind of involvement.

Photographs taken and processed by a group of 11 year old children in a school photography club.

Schools use photography for a number of different purposes:

- for enjoyment
- as support, recording and resource material for school projects, outings and expeditions
- to record school activities
- to illustrate and support personal interviews (for example, one group took photographs as part of a Police Liaison project)
- to record growth or seasonal change, nature study and science
- as a means of researching visual qualities (pattern, form, texture etc)
- to study movement
- to study character in human beings and animals
- for set assignments

Photograms are a useful experimental means of understanding photography and using the potential of images. To create photograms, objects and shapes of an opaque or semi-opaque nature are placed on light-sensitive paper and exposed to light. (A sheet of glass is a useful anchor for flat items.) Following initial experiment, designs can be built up and awareness of shape and space encouraged.

Schools can usually acquire old cameras from a variety of sources. A 35mm single lens reflex camera, together with a supply of black and white film and the necessary developing and printing materials is ideal. The simpler the first camera, the more thoroughly concentration can be given to the selection of imagery.

There is no need for very young children to understand how photography works before they use the camera (after all, they switch on electric lights without understanding electricity!), but as soon as they are interested and able to handle the camera with confidence the teacher can explain the technical skills. Looking at an empty camera, they can see how altering the 'f' number on the lens allows more or less light to come in, and they will see how speed change affects the shutter. They should also practise loading and unloading film. Focusing can be assisted by the use

of a tripod – setting the controls gives the children enough to think about, without having to hold the camera still as well. All experience in taking pictures should be carefully documented, recording type of film, 'f' number and shutter speed, so that the results can be discussed.

Developing A daylight loading tank is useful for teaching the routines of development. Children should practise rolling old pieces of film into the tank before they use the 'real thing'. The importance of time, temperature and agitation on the quality of the negatives cannot be over-stressed. Resin-coated papers are highly recommended as within a short time the children can have washed and dried prints ready for folders – to be displayed or taken home. Safety is a key factor in developing, and must always be stressed. Children should be taught to use tongs and to handle chemicals safely. Wet and dry areas of printing should be kept apart.

If more equipment is available children can experiment with flash photography, close-ups and filters, and with enlarging.

Many schools who have developed this curriculum area speak of the children's keen enthusiasm. In some cases, photography can deeply involve children who are difficult to interest in other ways. At its best, it can be a powerful means of research and learning, as well as the beginning of a possibly lifelong interest.

Chapter 5 The Relationship of Design and Art

*D*ESIGN EDUCATION in the early years is a relatively new concept and as such is in the throes of development for good or ill – depending on the understanding of the teachers concerned.

In September 1984 the Department of Trade and Industry funded research through the Design Council into the role of Design and primary education. Their terms of reference were: 'To propose to the Design Council the policies and views that should be adopted with respect to design-related activities in primary schools and to recommend the associated actions that should be taken by such organisations and individuals as may be appropriate.'

It is interesting to note that from the onset the term 'design-related activities' superseded design education, and it is on this crucially important point that an understanding of the nature of the experience hinges.

The working party went on to clarify further the meaning of 'design-related activities', stating: 'We are not proposing the introduction of a new subject, called design, into the primary curriculum. Instead, we wish to identify the opportunities which exist, within the normal pattern of primary school activity, and to develop children's capacity for design.'

As teachers we are much more aware than we were of the 'hidden curriculum' with its implicit values, and good primary education has always been aware of the cross-disciplinary nature of experience. Design and designing can be seen to be pertinent to a number of curriculum areas – the creative and aesthetic, mathematical, physical, scientific and linguistic in particular. This is sound theory, but what is design and how do we recognise it in the classroom?

We believe that human beings have been designing ever since they identified specific needs and responded to them – it is as basic as that! In so doing they gathered materials and ideas and rearranged and shaped them to fulfil their purposes. They did this in many different ways and their failures disintegrated and were lost – although hopefully the experience added to their understanding and enabled future successes!

Young children are by nature inventive and will quite naturally isolate problems and work at them (although this may not be isolated or translated into words at first). At the very heart of this development lies concentration on a way of thinking, working and problem solving which is practical, intuitive or logical as befits the challenge. It offers the child a very powerful educational tool which, if seen to be of cross-curricular relevance, enables personal initiative, thought, research and practice which is independent of teacher-led solutions. 'Successful attitudes are seldom the result of chance' state the Design Council Working Party; clearly the associated teaching will need to be far subtler and stronger than the setting of a problem to which there is a right or wrong answer.

If children are interested in and encouraged to experience and respond to the natural and manmade world, their understanding will deepen and their critical faculties develop. If they are encouraged to think for themselves, to experiment and envisage a variety of possible ways of developing ideas, they will be able to use initiative and to consider alternatives and improvements, evaluating the process and practice at the end of the procedure. If they are encouraged to work individually or in groups, initiatives and skills can be developed enabling them to find solutions to problems and putting their ideas into practice.

Art and design

Design-related activities pertaining to art and craft are innumerable. They cover the whole range of material-based play and practice from the nursery school onwards, and can be developed through two- and three-dimensional experiences. Painting, drawing, modelling, sculpture, construction, textiles, printmaking, bookmaking, calligraphy, all have a part to play, and groupwork can offer a rich vein of experience. Children need to handle materials in the way that adults do, experiencing wood, stone, clay, threads, fibres, metals and modern products in order to gain insight into their qualities and see potential for further uses.

Good designers/craftsmen know the characteristics of their raw materials intimately and can enhance and exploit inherent qualities to the full. The density, weathering and loadbearing qualities of stone affect the nature of design for purpose in buildings. The nature of particular woods – grain, flexibility and toughness – needs to be understood if a functional item such as a chair, or a wood block for print-making, is to be designed. Knowledge of threads and fibres is necessary in order to make fabrics for fashion, the home, protection, or industrial use. The same criterion is equally important in the world of modern and synthetic materials, if we are not to find ourselves with problems of collapsing buildings, dangerous household items or disintegrating fabrics!

Developing ideas, isolating (or being set) problems and considering ways in which to answer them, executing practical work and envisaging potential developments, are experiences which will run side by side in a lively classroom. Art education in the first years of schooling, with its fine balance between intuitive and logical modes of thinking, creativity, practice and evaluation, should form a sound basis for design experience. Key elements inherent in art education are:

- sensory experience
- attitude and initiative
- ability to work independently and develop ideas, isolate problems and deal with them
- ability to analyse and learn by visual and tactile means
- practical experience and awareness of the potential of line, shape, colour, pattern, texture, tone and form; of tools, materials and media; and of communication by graphic means
- ability to enjoy and respond critically and intelligently to art and design forms, past and present
- ability to use language in describing processes, developing discussion and evaluating ideas.

The design process most commonly in use in secondary and adult education consists of the following stages:

1 Consideration of the problem/challenge set. Analysis and search for relevant information and ideas.
2 Production of notes/sketches/mock-ups of a number of different solutions to the problem.
3 Evaluation of solutions. Selection of a plan of action.
4 Creation of an artefact/end product/form.
5 Final evaluation by the pupil, working with the teacher or other pupils.

Much of this process will prove inappropriate for a child in the first years of schooling. At worst, fostering understanding of the design process itself, or rigid adherence to the processes, could lead to less good design practice than direct, intuitive working in response to challenges (this would undoubtedly happen if the child were to be introduced to the process too early). At best, it could be simply a useful learning process. *It should always be remembered that there are as many alternative design processes as there are designs and designers.*

It is often possible for the adult designer to visualise and plan products in advance and work towards that end, separating the functions as previously defined. Many, however, work by other methods and means, in particular those who use an artist/craftsman approach. These designers work directly into materials, evolving, developing and modifying ideas through a series of pieces of work, through experiment, trial, error and success. In this context drafting, if it comes into the process at all, takes place in notating drawing, photography or computer design *at the end of the process.*

Examples of this way of working may be found among sculptors, potters, ceramics and textiles artist/designers, printmakers, fashion, stage and graphic designers. It is also to be found in the approach of some scientists and engineers. In Jack Cross's words, 'The artist cannot, must not know in advance exactly how his work will end. The demands of the medium, his own responses to it, the actual developing existence of the work in progress all operate to modify his evolving conception'. Although certainly not written with young children in mind this is very apt if we watch them at work building up paintings, print, using clay or constructing from found materials, to name but a few activities.

An alternative structure which could be appropriate to the needs of the child in the first years of schooling might be defined as follows:
- consideration of the problem/challenge set. Analysis, search for relevant information and ideas. Selection of materials.
- practical research and development of ideas through handling materials.
- culmination of practical research in an artefact/end product/form.
- annotating, drawing, recording, describing the process if appropriate.
- final evaluation by the child working with teachers and other children.

Any processes, or briefs constructed should enable and encourage better understanding and practice, and be seen to be means rather than ends in design education.

In evaluating their own practice, teachers would be well advised to consider four crucial questions

1 Do the design processes used enable children to develop practical/theoretical 'answers' to needs and problems through natural and direct ways of working, or are they hurdles to be overcome before effective designing can take place?
2 Is there a balance between personally motivated projects and challenges? (Are the children being enabled to follow their own personal needs and problems which evolve naturally from their own work in art and craft?)
3 Are the challenges/problems set of the kind which will enable children to respond in a genuinely original way? (It is possible to set projects which can only allow for a limited response, precluding any real invention or divergent thinking.)
4 Are the tools, materials and resources of an appropriate quality for good design experience to take place?

It is important that children are given opportunity to see and discuss interesting design through environmental and museum studies, looking at artefacts, and reproductions, fashion and clothing, toys, functional and decorated items, and advertisement, etc.

Some examples of practice are described below.

OPEN-ENDED PROBLEM SOLVING

'*See what you can do with these*' Such challenges will include all kinds of experimental work with materials – painting, drawing, modelling and construction, rigid material, collage, textiles etc. (See under section headings.)

In one example of this approach a teacher sectioned off part of the playground – ensuring adequate space for a group of children to work with a collection of begged, borrowed and acquired items with potential for construction such as bricks, wood blocks and lengths, rope etc. (It was not envisaged that the components would be fixed and therefore all items could be re-used or returned when finished with.)

DESIGN AND ART 1–2

The children were introduced to the materials and reminded about the need for safe handling and mutual sensitivity. Following the 'What can you do with these' challenge and general discussion the children naturally moved into work situations,

Playground construction.

Construction and skills.

some individually and others co-operatively. In the latter it was noticeable that there were times of coming together followed by periods of working alone. Great decision making moments were apparent with children holding objects over their constructions in several different positions before gently lowering them, or before rejecting them and selecting other pieces. Positive encouragement and praise was given by the teacher together with additional challenges and questioning when the time was deemed right.

The very nature of the materials continually triggered new ideas and associations and many of the problems encountered were generated by the children in the course of the work. These were faced and worked through with determination, only occasionally needing sensitive teacher support in the form of relevant questions and encouragement. This experience could be seen as an introduction to creative practical problem solving, supported by the build-up of relevant skills. It could also be developed further as a learning process through practical work, discussion and projection of hypothetical problems by the children. Recording skills could be developed through drawings, diagrams and words as appropriate to the nature of the projects.

In addition, the approach provides valuable experience of the discipline imposed by materials and tools – leading to an understanding of appropriate qualities and the importance of safe handling of tools and equipment.

SEARCH AND RESEARCH

This approach is a crucial component not only of art and design education but of the whole curriculum. It is based on first-hand experience and second-hand evidence and stands or falls on the teacher's vision, provision, motivating power and expectation.

Looking at the environment

Children's investigations into the natural and manmade environment could focus on one or more of the following areas:

Materials
- earth/clay, stone, slate, wood, pigments, fibres, concrete, ceramic, metal etc.
- experimenting with materials, and their potential usage

The built environment
- city, town, village, school, house, church, factory etc
- looking at function, planning, arrangements . . .
- investigating how a specific material has been used

Building and constructions – windows, doors, chimneys, drainpipes, pylons, aerials, fences, roofing materials, surfaces etc.

Patterns in buildings – bricks, tiles, surfaces, pavements . . .

Energy generation – wind and water generating machinery (wind and water mills, solar heating equipment . . .)

Functional machinery cranes, pylons, radar, farm, garden, road construction

Domestic appliances kitchen utensils, telephone, electrical equipment

Furniture (past and present) – form, function and decoration

Receptacles and containers – road, rail and sea, food packaging, drinking and eating receptacles (cups, mugs, jugs, tea and coffee pots, bottles etc) – design and usage, materials used . . .

Tools
- drawing and writing tools past and present . . .
- cutting tools, knives, scissors; measuring tools – rules, set squares, dividers, compasses . . . ; handtools – hammers, planes, screwdrivers, saws etc.
- handles . . .
- making primitive tools and testing them . . .

Toys of all kinds – purpose, form, function and decoration

Textiles – clothing (past and present – climatic problems). Searching for specific materials, wood, cotton, manmade, plastic, leather etc. Design and purpose . . .

Throughout these experiences questions will constantly arise, for example:

Why was this made in this way . . . ?
What do you think of it? What is it made of?
What does it look/feel like or remind you of?
Will it work? Will it do the job it is intended for?
Is it a good design? Why?/Why not?
How could it be improved?

DEFINED PROBLEM
SOLVING

Design briefs can be introduced in spoken or written form. Ideas for interesting design challenges include:

Working models – bridges, wind appliances and wheels

Vehicles, boats etc (see the *Raft project* on page 172)

Buildings for specific purposes, shelters (see page 170)

Lifting gear, fun machines and inventions.

Constructions of specified dimensions; machinery or load-bearing items which can be tested

Good design and construction for specified content

Containers and receptacles for a specified purpose

Packaging for a purpose

Decoration for a purpose

Changing the environment or part of it for a purpose

Furnishing – home, 'home corners', parts of the school – curtains, cushions

Fashion – clothing, decoration, patterning

Sets and costumes – for projects and plays

Posters and pictures to communicate specific messages

Puppetry to communicate a specific story/happening

Decorative map making – journey to school – treasure island – hazards and safety aspects . . .

Labelling and lettering for specific needs

Building models as part of a play area – space ship cockpit, giraffe, maze, iron man, prehistoric monster, Viking ship etc . . .

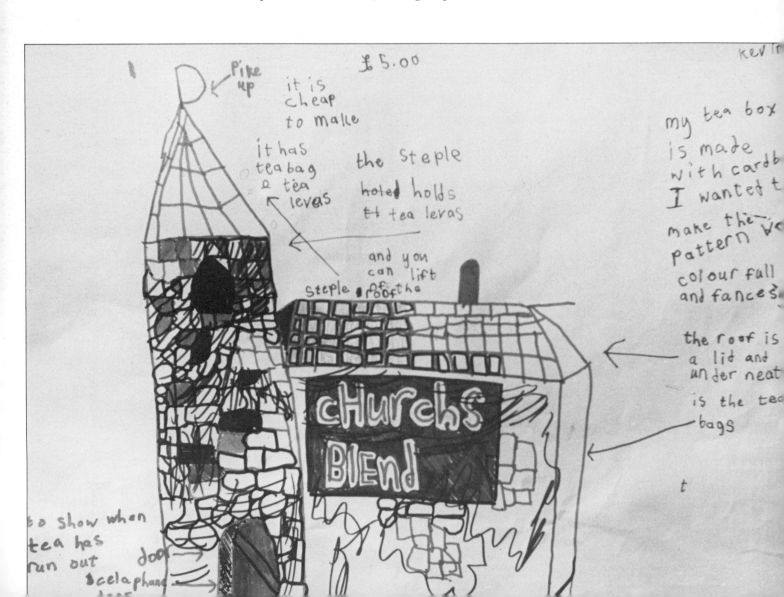

Tea Container
'Special presentation'

These photographs show the outcome of a design brief. The pupil was challenged to design and make a 'special presentation tea container' based on the topic of buildings in the locality. The child's thinking and planning can clearly be seen, together with the string block, designed to add decoration to the finished item (the church door was infilled with red polythene in order to see when the packet was low, or empty).

Other aspects and examples of design and designing appear throughout Section 1 (curriculum planning and content, areas of experience, groupwork and photography) and in Section 2 under the headings of 'claywork', 'art and garden project', 'weddings', 'tortoise project', 'guinea pig', 'raft', 'pantomime' and 'shelter projects', 'snowman' (groupwork), 'church project', 'Bigods Suffolk', 'Medieval pot pourri' and 'design for cards'.

Chapter 6 Some aspects of art for children with special educational needs

*T*HE TERM 'special educational needs' in this context covers the whole range of physical and mental handicap, emotional disturbance, slow learning and deprivation, together with uneven development and giftedness. Clearly, with such a range it will only be possible to offer very general considerations, and we are only too aware that much of what is said will be inappropriate for some children.

Children are individuals with an incredibly wide range of problems and abilities. Good teachers will take pains to accept and understand each child and to assess the stage he or she has reached, prior to planning future experience and development.

We believe that the general approach outlined in this book is relevant to all children – with its threefold structure based on sensory and media experience, together with appropriate expectation. With regard to the latter, there are a number of well-documented case studies of very seriously handicapped children and adults being able to excel in some aspects which, at first sight, would seem improbable or even impossible.

The way in which this general approach is handled, and the emphasis placed on certain parts of the art curriculum, or on specific stages of development, will depend on the nature of the special need. It is understood that for many severely handicapped children it may not be possible to go further than sensory awareness and the experience of different qualities against the skin. Gifted children (who may not be gifted in art) will need a programme which offers balance and introduces them to the creative/aesthetic aspects of the curriculum, both practically and theoretically.

The main difference between handicapped children and their so-called 'normal' peers may well be in the age at which their ability, understanding and practice fits into the generally-accepted pattern of sequential development. In adolescence, mentally-handicapped youngsters may be at the scribble stage or at an early symbolist mode of working. It is very important that they should be gently extended in every way possible *appropriate to the stage reached*. Use of interesting graphic tools, rich colour, malleable clay and other basic materials will offer stimulation and extend experience. The teacher's main aim will be to interest the children and to extend their potential by involving them in experiences of value, being careful not to outface them or to inhibit their development.

It is possible for children to suffer from the effects of a pattern of expectations imposed on them by parents, relatives (and, on occasions, teachers) regarding art activities. They may be led to the conclusion that their own work is of little value, or is inferior, because it has been judged in the light of so-called 'acceptable art' – which almost always means art in a representational form. The children are therefore deprived of the fulfilment and pleasure which can derive from the equally important aspects of pattern, colour, shape, line, form etc. It must be remembered that much adult art is abstract; many designers of surfaces and fabrics, for example, work entirely in the mode of pattern. Moreover, a large number of the world's children do not draw or model 'likenesses' because their religious beliefs forbid this. Clearly, there are possibilities for rich experience outside the realm of representation.

Becoming aware of a rich variety of art forms of all kinds – especially pattern and abstract works – is an important and enjoyable part of the child's experience. Down's Syndrome children especially seem to enjoy intricate patterning. It is crucially important, too, that teachers realise the need to stimulate children's imagination by surrounding them with, and introducing them to, reality. A child kept in a restricted space, without visual or tactile stimuli, human or animal company, would have little for the imagination to feed on, and would be very severely deprived. Introduction to the whole environment, to artefacts and art forms, through sensory experience, is a powerful basis for education.

Reference is often made to the psychological effects of colour and this is used to effect by contemporary interior designers. It is sometimes useful – and certainly interesting – to experiment with pupils by offering restricted palettes, colour displays or even whole environments in relation to behaviour patterns, in order to assess pleasurable or adverse responses, or changes in regard to hyperactivity or stimulation of withdrawn children.

Many mentally handicapped children can enjoy colour, shape, texture, pattern and form in its own right. Indeed, some can only be described as gifted – organisation, balance, harmony and skill being clearly apparent. In *Lives worth living* Elizabeth Marais describes a Downes Syndrome boy who could respond in this way, in spite of his very poor motor control and coordination. The joy of handling colour, materials and malleable substances for their own sake, when not inhibited by a requirement for 'realistic content', allows for reward and fulfilment as well as learning, whether or not there appears to be an 'end product'. Visual and kinaesthetic experience will no doubt play a considerable part in this enjoyment.

Children with special educational needs very often require more experience of play and experimentation with materials than their peers and this process should be encouraged and extended. The sensitive teacher will continually monitor the child's response to various tools, materials and ways of working, in order to find out what is most appropriate in helping to assist that child's development. Physical problems should be noted and, where possible, alternative materials and modified tools introduced to help compensate.

Paint can prove to be a liberation for some children; oil pastels, with their potential for strong marks and rich colours, may be wonderfully rewarding for pupils with poor motor skills and coordination. Somewhat surprisingly, fine line tools have provided the point of breakthrough for some children with these problems; broad hog-hair brushes, sponges and printmaking items offer useful drawing tools for others. It is interesting to note that some partially sighted and blind children respond very positively to graphic tools and paint, and can, surprisingly, build up vigorous work with strong images.

Malleable substances like dough, clay or plasticine offer direct, sensory experiences. For some children this fundamental form of three-dimensional work can be developed to a high degree of originality and skill. In some cases, this leads naturally into two-dimensional or relief work. Textiles and collage offer unique textural experience which can be enjoyed by children with severe visual, or even manipulative, problems. Strong warps can be set up on large weaving frames and woven with wools, threads and scraps of material and paper.

Children enjoy making rubbings and seeing fascinating images emerge. Creating such highly-acceptable patterns can help build up their confidence. Rubbing patterns can be further developed through overlaying and flooding, or used as a basis for collage and paint, as well as in the context of design.

Children who are undergoing emotional difficulties resulting from a mismatch of ideas and the abilities to carry them out will require much experience of handling tools and materials. They will also need to be sensitively reorientated as regards their own expectations and helped to build up looking, touching and selecting skills.

Highly-gifted children will also benefit from this kind of approach. They may well move quickly or directly into intricate pattern and design making, or into the analytic phase, bypassing some or all of the other stages. They too should be encouraged and extended in every possible way, and should be challenged to further their own enquiries and experimentation – for example, by studying interesting items, looking at artists' and craftsmen's work, using a sketchbook to make drawings at home and out of school. No child need be frustrated in his or her development providing the teacher can arouse their interest in the rich variety apparent in the natural and

118

Drawings by children in a Special School, spanning a wide age range.

manmade world, and in the potential of searching, recording, designing, expressing and modifying. Sequences of development in one area of experience will be found to be more satisfactory than 'butterflying' from one activity to another in a series of superficial 'tastings', as children learn to work through difficulties, and control and use ideas and media to their own ends.

If a child has reached a very different stage of development from the rest of the peer group, it is important that he or she has the opportunity to see work of an appropriate level from a different age group or school, so that a reasonable 'norm' is introduced and possibilities are offered for extending experience. It is always important to search for areas of experience at which children can succeed. A group of children suffering from cerebral palsy were introduced to the work of Expressionists and Post-Impressionists. For the first time, they realised that there were images which depended upon broken lines for their vibrance and vitality. It is not surprising that they had considered their own efforts failures, given their previously accepted 'norm' – built up from looking at hard-edged or photographic imagery. Drawings following this experience showed confidence, vigour, sensitivity in colour and line, and considerable personal involvement.

Problems and failures should always be considered as interesting challenges to overcome, rather than disasters to be forgotten. It is important that teachers monitor individual children in order to assess difficulties and development. A collection of the child's work, kept in chronological order in a folder, will prove to be an invaluable diagnostic tool, as well as offering appropriate information on which to base further teaching. It is also valuable for the child to see a body of his or her own work and to be able to discuss it with the teacher.

Teacher or parent beliefs that children have no imagination or that art is a gift which we have – or have not – got, are misconceptions. Clearly, there are different levels of ability (and we all have our own remedial areas!) but imagination and worthwhile art experience can be fostered and enabled to develop in all children.

Trees. Boy. 10 years. Powder colour and wax crayon. 600 × 450 mms.

Chapter 7 Evaluation, Monitoring and Assessment

*E*VALUATION, monitoring and assessment should be seen in context of the quality of education we offer our children. The function of evaluation is to improve educational practice by:

- looking at our own planning and performance as teachers;
- looking at the understanding and performance of the child;
- encouraging the child to look at his own approach, performance and practice.

Our own appraisal should lead us to consider aims and objectives in the light of practice and of the child's understanding and response to these objectives (see page 34 on 'Role of Teacher'). *Evaluation* is literally considering the worth, or value of the education we offer. *Monitoring* pertains to the means and organisational ploys brought to bear on the subject or individual to be considered. *Assessment* is to do with practice and performance, and will involve a number of differing criteria for making judgements as to whether certain qualities are apparent, or if change and development is evident. In practice, the three aspects are interrelated, and must be seen as a whole.

In order to evaluate, it is important to find an appropriate means of monitoring the child's programme and progress through the class and during his whole school career. This will mean close liaison between teachers in a school, so that there is understanding, communication, reporting and cooperation between schools and continuity is maintained.

Some kind of record keeping will be necessary, but the method and content should be carefully considered: much time and energy can be wasted by complicated systems which offer very little real information in the final analysis. Comments such as 'good', or 'satisfactory' are meaningless unless there is knowledge of the quality of practice of the teacher, as well as an understanding of the criteria on which they were based.

All forms of marking eg, numeral and literal grades should be rejected at this stage, as they can only take into account judgements of particular aspects of end product assessment, or offer highly subjective views which have little to do with overall development and are equally inappropriate.

In the first years of schooling our aim is to enable children to think and act for themselves, to be resilient enough to work in many different ways and to build up understanding, practical development and skills. It is therefore necessary for teachers to keep a close watch on individuals, noting response, attitude and involvement in order to assess their own effectiveness in teaching.

It will also be helpful to assess the body of work built up by the child over a period of time. Unless a child's work is seen in sequence, it is not possible for any real judgement to be made regarding development. This may well cause teachers to reappraise the practice of sending most pieces of practical work home. There are times when this is appropriate, but there must be sufficient work for the teacher to monitor the child's development. The following excerpts from the Schools Council's publication *Children's Growth through Creative Experience* (1978) are of interest in this context:

Art Education is concerned with the creative growth of the child and it follows from this that progress is made when the child widens his experience. Children's work cannot therefore be assessed over a short period, and progress should be looked for over a term, or over a year rather than month by month. The growth of technical skills is only one criterion. Progress also becomes apparent as the child acquires increasing sensitivity to pattern and colour, and awareness about the way in which forms and mechanisms operate, and a growing capacity to evolve images which combine personal meaning with the power to affect others . . . we believe that . . . a child's work can be criticised and assessed taking into account the child himself, and what he is capable of. Sincerity is the essential criterion, the work should be a genuine personal statement or response to the imaginative situation or problem and for the degree of involvement. Thirdly, and particularly with older children, the teacher may assess the way materials and tools have been used, the approach to the problem and the kind of technical or inventive solution that has been found.

The manner in which we convey our assessment or evaluation of children's work is important. The child will be quick to sense negative attitudes and judgements even when they are not spoken. Positive encouragement and challenge can change and develop standards more than negative criticism but the child will not respect lax approval.

In the early stages young children work directly and often quickly; although deeply involved at the time, they no longer identify themselves with 'the product' when it is finished. It is therefore inappropriate to expect them to make alterations or develop work at this stage. No doubt the teacher will note areas to be developed when assessment is taking place, and plan future challenges accordingly.

Record cards should offer the kind of information which is of genuine use in profiling the child, or in considering future programmes. These, together with examples of work, can form an excellent basis for the next teacher and can save much time in building up an understanding of the pupil and diagnosing his stage of development. Figures 7.1–7.3 show examples of record cards used in Suffolk Education Authority.

It is valuable for children to be able to look through a sequence of their own work and to discuss it with teachers. Where this has been practised, interesting and often surprising insights into motivation and understanding have been gained. In the final analysis, monitoring and assessment should lead to a demonstration of change of practice and evidence of understanding on the part of the pupils, if their education has been effective. Teachers will be continually evaluating the nature of that change as part of the teaching programme and will no doubt consider their own responsibilities in light of it.

Figure 7.1

Example of a record card.   **Suffolk Education Authority**

Name ....   School ....

Age ....Class ....   Date ....

BALANCE OF COURSE COVERED

Drawing	Colour	Painting	Printmaking
Textiles	3D work	Collage	Response to artefacts

PREDOMINANT STAGE REACHED   SCRIBBLE   SYMBOLIST   ANALYST

RESPONSE.   ATTITUDES.   INVOLVEMENT.

RELEVANT LIKES AND DISLIKES

Ability to   Work independently

               Work spontaneously

               Overcome difficulties

Response to Resources

Quality of Observational Skills

Particular Strengths and Weaknesses

Development Apparent

Triggers for Future Teaching

This may be copied for use in schools

Figure 7.2

Examples of a record card   Suffolk Education Authority

Name **RUPERT ROPER**   School — **Primary School**

Age **8 : 4**   Class **3**   Date **SUMMER TERM 1987**

BALANCE OF COURSE COVERED

Drawing	✓	Colour	✓	Painting	✓	Printmaking	✓
Textiles		3D work	✓	Collage		Response to artefacts	✓

PREDOMINANT STAGE REACHED   SCRIBBLE   (SYMBOLIST) ➔ ANALYST

RESPONSE. ATTITUDES. INVOLVEMENT.
Lengthy concentration and involvement in any activities undertaken. Obsession with stones — making collections, and experimenting with colour, pattern, texturing, and matching.

RELEVANT LIKES AND DISLIKES   He enjoys two dimensional work, but is less responsive to three dimensional modelling & junk construction.

Ability to   Work independently   Excellent. He uses his own initiative.

Work spontaneously   Only in response to his own stimuli (stones)

Overcome difficulties   Needs reassurance but is able to work through difficulties.

Response to Resources   Limited unless given strong stimulation and challenge.

Quality of Observational Skills   Keen. He will often return to an object many times. Qualities of real looking apparent

Particular Strengths and Weaknesses   Often limits his work to areas in which he is sure of success. Within this range there is some very interesting thinking and practice.

Development Apparent   The quality of marks made with graphic tools. Experience of paint, — mixing and matching. Analytical skills.

Triggers for Future Teaching   Encouragement to broaden his field of experience (including textiles.) Use of clay to stimulate a three dimensional response.

This may be copied for use in schools   Introduction to reproductions of 'Colourists' 'primitives' and illuminated manuscript letters to extend experience.

Figure 7.3

Examples of a record card   Suffolk Education Authority

Name *DAVID DAMION* .... School *— PRIMARY SCHOOL* ....

Age ...*6.1*...... Class ...*I*............ Date *SUMMER TERM 1987* .....

BALANCE OF COURSE COVERED

Drawing	✓	Colour	✓	Painting		Printmaking	✓
Textiles		3D work		Collage	✓	Response to artefacts	✓

PREDOMINANT STAGE REACHED   SCRIBBLE → (SYMBOLIST)→   ANALYST

RESPONSE. ATTITUDES. INVOLVEMENT.

WELL MOTIVATED, LIVELY AND INTERESTED.

RELEVANT LIKES AND DISLIKES *ENJOYS FINE WORK AND DRAWING. DOES NOT APPRECIATE PAINTING OR USING LARGER TOOLS.*

Ability to   Work independently *ON SOME OCCASIONS HIS INVOLVEMENT IS TOTAL.*

Work spontaneously *HE NEEDS A STARTING POINT FROM WHICH TO WORK.*

Overcome difficulties *HE CAN AT TIMES BECOME DESPONDENT WHEN HIS GOALS ARE NOT IN SIGHT.*

Response to Resources *HE ENJOYS WORKING FROM FIRST HAND STIMULI AND IS ABLE TO QUESTION AND EXPERIMENT FROM THIS BASE.*

Quality of Observational Skills *HIS SYMBOLIC STYLE IS ANGULAR AND SQUARE; THIS HAS AN EFFECT ON HIS OBSERVATIONAL INTERPRETATION. HE IS MOVING TOWARD AN ANALYSIS OF DETAIL.*

Particular Strengths and Weaknesses *COLLAGE, ENJOYMENT OF SHAPE AND TEXTURAL QUALITIES ARE A GREAT DELIGHT. PRINTMAKING IS AT THE RANDOM STAGE, AND DOES NOT APPEAR TO HAVE DEVELOPED.*

Development Apparent *DRAWING, TEXTURAL QUALITIES AND THE ABILITY TO USE COLOURS EFFECTIVELY RATHER THAN IN A HAPHAZARD FASHION.*

Triggers for Future Teaching *CONSTANT ENCOURAGEMENT TO WORK THROUGH PROBLEMS: CHALLENGE TO WORK IN THREE DIMENSIONS: EMPHASIS ON PATTERN AND DETAIL: BUILD-UP OF OBSERVATIONAL SKILLS. TEXTILE EXPERIENCE.*

This may be copied for use in schools

Some authorities have experimented with self-report sheets (see Figure 7.4). These can prove enlightening and interesting to the teacher as well as to the child. Thoughts about the work and the teacher's approach can be made explicit and insights provided into interest, motivation and difficulties. Care should be taken, however, over making self-analysis a regular feature as too much introversion at too early an age can rob experiences of non-verbal qualitative response and spontaneity.

Figure 7.4

Name . . . .**Class** . . . .**Date** . . . .

1   Describe the work you have been doing:
    (title or project)

2   Say why you did or did not enjoy doing it?

3   Why were you pleased, or not pleased with it?

4   How could it have been better?

5   What have you learned by doing it?

Chapter 8 Environment for Learning

SOME AUTHORITIES suggest that at least 60% of learning takes place by visual means. Clearly a significant proportion of our experience is assimilated through the senses of sight and touch, whatever the actual proportion; the whole matter of visual and tactile communication is, therefore, of crucial importance in the education of children.

It is necessary for the teacher to become visually literate and to understand how children learn through the experience of seeing and touching, as well as having a working knowledge of the skills of presentation. Leadership in the whole matter of visual awareness, communication and display may come from the headteacher, or from a member of staff who has the responsibility with or without a defined post. It is too important a matter to be left to haphazard personal intiative, and must be part of a carefully considered school policy.

The whole quality of the school environment, its mode of organisation and display, can enhance or actually inhibit learning and can build or erode the child's understanding of whether his work is valued or of little real importance. It is an opportunity to set the scene for consideration and care of the environment and the things within it. If our own organisation and presentation is poor we quickly communicate to children a lack of pride in what we do and an acceptance of low standards. It is not an overstatement to say that this often leads to carelessness on the part of the child or even to thoughtless vandalism.

The physical environment

Education is concerned with the whole child. The environment in which we place that child, by law, for at least five hours a day, five days a week for a large part of each year, needs careful consideration. This is the background for learning and is, indeed, part of it.

Schools and their environs vary greatly and some lend themselves more readily than others to providing a conducive background for learning. However, with ingenuity much can be done. A working party of members of staff viewing the building and its environs with a fresh eye can often generate ideas for development. A disciplined approach, somewhat like a 'Time and Motion' study, which takes into consideration the nature of the work, the philosophy of the school, and the 'fixed points' (toilets, sinks, dining areas, etc) is a useful start. If an overall plan of campaign is then drawn up and costed, it can be systematically put into practice over a period of time as finances permit (although it is surprising what can be done for very little outlay in many instances).

THE EXTERIOR AND GROUNDS

The layout of the grounds and their upkeep is not usually the province of the school teaching staff, nevertheless considerable influence and initiative can be brought to bear on these aspects. Playground equipment or play sculpture may be installed, seats carefully placed, interesting plants or shrubs introduced. Sand areas or out of door work areas for construction or modelling in good weather may be set up, while the whole question of a nature environment is one which has successfully exercised a number of schools. Sculptural forms (free-standing or relief) designed and made by the children, or purchased by the school from artists and craftsmen, can also be introduced. (Regional Arts Associations have assisted financially in a number of school projects of this kind and Parent Teacher Associations and other interested bodies are often willing to contribute.)

THE INTERIOR
COMMUNAL SPACE

'Many headteachers now feel that children should encounter in school a stimulating visual environment as an essential part of their education . . .'
(Schools Council 1974, *Art and Design in the Middle Years of Schooling*)

A starting point in considering the interior of the school buildings might well be to take a careful look at the ways of entry into the building for children, staff and visitors. What messages do we convey in these areas regarding the school and its philosophy? Are there wall spaces which could be utilised for display purposes? High level displays are acceptable providing the items are of a nature to be seen from a distance. Areas of pinboard can transform walls, and do not need to be framed with moulding unless they are at levels where edges may become worn or frayed.

Proceeding through the school corridors, stairways, cloakrooms or communal areas, colour should be taken into consideration. A bright, clean atmosphere is a top priority, with warm shades in cold areas. In choosing colours for wall boards etc it is important to think of the items to be displayed – strong colours can overpower or devalue what is to be communicated. Fabrics, carpeted areas, seats, cushions, plants and other interesting items can all make a positive contribution.

Some financial outlay on a good display screen assemblage is well worth considering. These are initially expensive, but will last for many years if handled with care and can be built up over a period of time, unit by unit.

Murals, reliefs and textile hangings can be designed for specific areas and can often meet the challenge of odd shapes; for example, a vertical area 240cm (8ft) × 60cm (2ft) might hold a variety of subjects – towers, beanstalks, totem poles, or even thin men! These can be reasonably long-term exhibits, or may be changed more frequently.

It is possible to mount hardboard panels on to walls with rawl plugs or on batons (see figure 8.1). These can be taken down and repainted as often as required, by children who enjoy working in groups. These have a 'finished' permanent quality, as they become part of the building, in spite of the possibility for change of subject matter at any time.

Textile hangings, woven, appliquéd, collaged or ceramic panels or units can also be designed for specific spaces. Collections of offcuts of material can be built up for use as background to displays.

Figure 8.1 (Hardboard panels in sliding grooves)

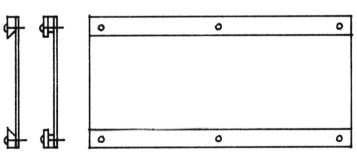
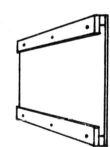

The content, design and practical aspects of these panels should be entirely the children's own work, although the teacher will have been the catalyst and enabler, providing challenge, stimulus, materials, advice and encouragement. The work will need planning, but it is not necessary, nor deemed appropriate, for the teacher to draft the work for the children to fill in.

Three-dimensional displays require firm shelving, table or bench tops, or a variety of stands or boxes, some for floor level displays. Improvisation will play a major part, but some firm structures are especially worth considering, as described below.

1 *Aluminium track with adjustable brackets and shelves* (Figure 8.2) makes a versatile display unit. If the wall behind these units is backed with pinboard, the result is a versatile piece of display equipment. Two-dimensional work can be fixed to the pinboard when the shelves are not in use. Three-dimensional work can be displayed on the shelves and mobiles or textiles can be suspended from the brackets.

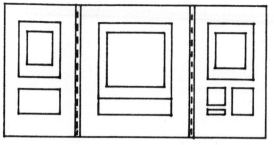
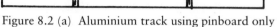
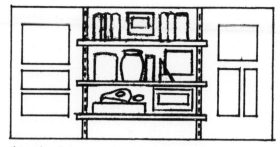

Figure 8.2 (a) Aluminium track using pinboard only   (b) Aluminium track with shelves and pinboard

2 *Sets of boxes* fitting one within another can be made of hardboard, softboard or plywood (see Figure 8.3) This idea can extend to carefully selected and cut cardboard packing cases, emulsion painted in neutral, black or white.

Figure 8.3

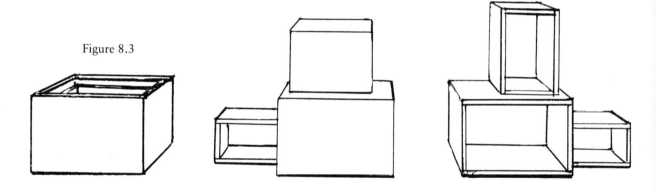

These units can be used in a number of ways for the display of three dimensional items and will store as a single unit within the largest rectangle.

3 *Bricks and thermalite blocks* can be used in a variety of ways for mounting three-dimensional items or for constructing bases for 'shelves' in displays.

4 *Corrugated card* can be obtained in rolls of varying height and can be used in a number of ways to form a background for displays. Work is attached to the fluted side of the roll by dressmakers' pins. In order to be firmly fixed the pins must be inserted carefully, vertically down or up the flute, and should not pierce through to the back of the paper.

Figures 8.4–8.8 illustrate different arrangements of card.

Figure 8.4

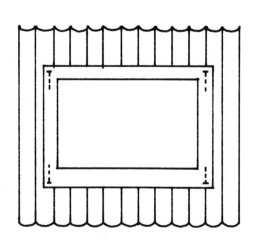

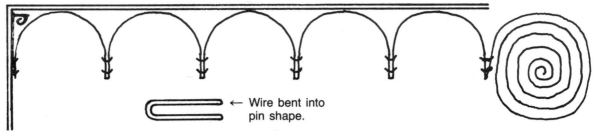

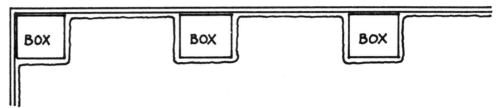

← Wire bent into pin shape.

Figure 8.5 Bays. *The card is held in position by bent wire, and dressmakers' pins are pushed down the flutes at the top and up the flutes at the bottom.*

Figure 8.6 Card is stapled onto structures – cupboards, tables, boxes, etc.

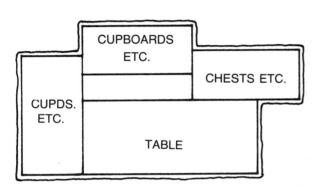

Figure 8.7 'Unwanted' furniture etc., can be built into an 'island' and surrounded by card to be made into an effective display unit for open days, parents meetings, etc.

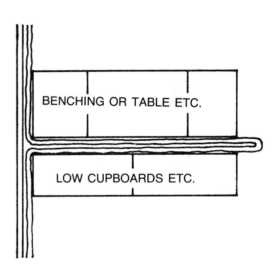

Figure 8.8 Room dividers held by furniture structures.

THE CLASSROOM

'The atmosphere of every room is a product of the interest and activities of pupils and teachers, but probably above everything else it is dependent upon the sensitivity of the teacher.'

(Kenneth Jamieson, *Junior School Art*)

The atmosphere of the room in which children spend most of their working day is of great importance. In all rooms there will be the problems of a multi-activity space with a lot of children, materials, equipment, books and stimuli resources to house. It is not easy to solve, but there are some considerations which might help.

In considering *space* it is of prime importance to look carefully at the activities the children will be undertaking and necessary movements in relation to them and the fixed points, such as water supply (or route to it), doors, cupboards, etc. Is our organisation of tools, materials, etc, logical, in relationship to the seating arrangement? Very often it is necessary to totally reappraise the organisation.

Arrangements of furniture, desks and tables will, no doubt, vary depending on the activities undertaken, but are there any space saving arrangements which perhaps have not been considered, for example, placing of a teacher's table or desk, or some children's desks, with one side against a wall? Grouped tables and desks will, of course, take less working space than single units and a variety of arrangements are worth considering.

Have the children got appropriate surfaces to work on? Clearly each child will need reasonable space with suitable furniture for activities such as reading and writing, but what of art activity? Are there easels or table tops suitable for children to stand at? What of the child who likes to sit and draw? In many cases it is apparent when looking at children drawing, that the child is too close to the work surface to really see what he or she is doing. Drawing boards made from plywood or hardboard, placed at an angle on the child's knees and resting against the bench or the table, can overcome this problem.

A general rule regarding drawing is to look at the children as they work. If they are sitting so close to what they are doing that they cannot appraise the work as a whole, the situation needs to be examined.

One possibility which might help in extending valuable working space is to construct worktops which hinge down against the wall when not in use (Figure 8.9).

Figure 8.9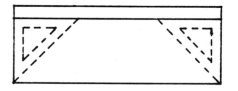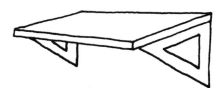

Display space within the classroom should be extended as far as possible with pinboarding on all available walls. In some instances it is realistic to panel the backs of doors and cupboards. In the short term, panels of corrugated card can be fixed to surfaces.

'Sympathetically arranged and sited displays all help to create a school 'tone' and form the backdrop for an educational philosophy which regards the enrichment of visual and tactile awareness in children as a vital priority'. (*Resources for Visual Education* 7–13, Schools Council Art Committee 1981).

There are a number of ways in which schools organise their display and visual communication, but the need for a coordinating influence is paramount. The Headteacher or designated teacher will need to lead, enthuse and coordinate other members of staff, parents and children, as well as organising in-school in-service courses to develop appropriate skills and sensitivities. Examples of practice include:
1 Dividing the general areas into sections, with teachers or year groups being responsible for specific areas on an agreed timetable, and reappraisal taking place periodically.
2 A main display area in the school being the responsibility of a rota of teachers, parents, teachers' aids and children. (In one school, the parents offered very interesting exhibitions – from travel souvenirs to colour displays, bottled fruit to fossils!).
3 Working on a common theme or project.
4 Building a core display as part of an experience to launch a school project.

PURPOSES OF DISPLAY

Display of resource material and children's work offers opportunities to build up the skills of learning and understanding and to enrich experience through visual means. It is not only a powerful tool to stimulate interest and thinking but also the basis for creative and aesthetic awareness.

Display can be seen as a fundamental non-verbal form of communication *a*) between teacher and pupil, where it can build up an understanding of aesthetic quality through experience as well as imparting much information; *b*) between the pupils and the teacher and other adults or peers.

As children are led towards the skills of seeing as opposed to scanning or haphazard looking, they will build up experiences which have a bearing on many life skills. These include independent analysis of objects and of the natural and man made world; the ability to read and understand diagrams, charts and visual aids; intelligent consideration of advertisements or posters and the use of stimulating material to develop independent creative work. It is interesting to note that movements as diverse as the early Christian Church and the Communist Movement in China understood the power of learning through the 'visual aid' and the .use of 'images' in order to illumine or consolidate their teaching.

In the case of the children's own work it is important to give them the opportunity to stand back and evaluate it for what it is. The fact that it has been mounted and displayed clearly communicates the fact that it is valued. The benefit of the cross-fertilisation of ideas through visual means in seeing one another's work is important, too. Many teachers will freely admit that their own thinking and practice is triggered into fresh channels and extended through seeing other people's classroom displays and children's work.

POINTS TO CONSIDER

The whole school is a potential visual aid and learning environment for the child. Simplicity is the keyword to success. The simpler and more straightforward the structure and layout of the display, the easier it will be to assimilate. The human brain becomes confused and 'turns off' if faced with too much jumbled information. The way items are arranged and mounted is also important. Human beings (as well as some animals, according to Desmond Morris) will show marked preference for order and symmetry over random patterning. Work hung at a variety of angles and trimmed to odd shapes or drawings mounted by cutting closely around the subject matter, are difficult to 'read' and this very often detracts from the content and value of the work.

Colour can have a very profound effect and can either enhance or inhibit learning. Sensitive choice of colours on display boards and mounts can set off the subtleties of colour within the work. Generally, neutral shades allow the colours within the work to 'speak for themselves' whilst garish hues deaden or harden them.

Display techniques

WALL DISPLAY

Mounting. Use a minimum of suitable adhesive with little or no water content. It is usually sufficient to smear a small amount within a half inch of the edges of the item to be mounted and at corners. Press from the centre outwards, having protected the surface with a spare sheet of paper. Any excess of adhesive will distort the paper.

Double mounting is desirable for certain occasions. Work need not be stuck to the mount (which can be used again) but can be mounted directly onto the wall with dressmaker's pins.

The visual effect is improved if the bottom margin is slightly wider than the top. In double mounting the outer mount margin will, in most cases, look better if it is wider than the inner mount.

When displaying writing it is useful to have shown some forethought in the manner in which the children were going to present the work. Many junior children need lines and there are many good papers solid enough to write clearly on but thin enough to show a line grid or even a sheet of file paper. The grid can be ruled for margins on each side and the child can then use this on many occasions (Figure 8.10 (a) (b) (c) (d)). In the case of a double page, the two inner margins equal one outer margin.

Figure 8.10 (a)   *(b)*   *(c)*   *(d)*

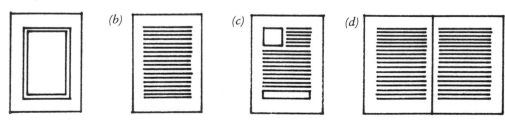

Arrangement of two-dimensional items
Work should be arranged so that horizontal and vertical edges are aligned where possible (Figure 8.11, 8.12).

Figure 8.11

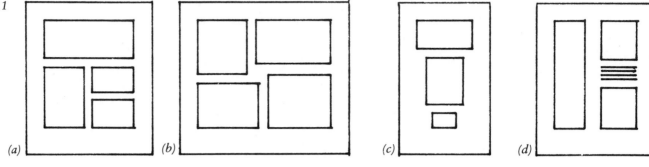

(a)   (b)   (c)   (d)

Figure 8.12

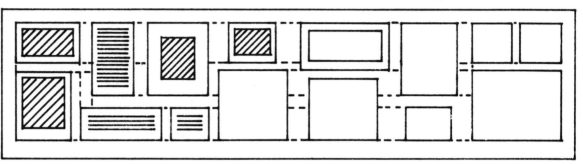

Note At the end of a day, when work is finished and ready for appraisal and discussion it can be useful to stage a *pavement show*. This can be set up on the classroom floor or in a nearby corridor. Clean sugar paper of a chosen colour can be carefully laid out and the work laid on to it. This will take a very few moments and enables all the children to look at the work immediately after it is finished and apparently mounted. (The horizontals and verticals of the arrangement are equally important in this situation.)

Fabric Lengths of fabric can be arranged effectively to hang in folds by cutting a width of paper (sugar paperweight) approximately 5cm deep × the width of the cloth and pinning it to the top, turning over the frayed edge. (The pins should be vertical.) This is an excellent way of taking the strain off fabrics when hanging, as pin-holes may otherwise damage the cloth (Figure 8.13). It will then be a simple matter to arrange the folds as desired and pin up the work.

Figure 8.13   (a)   (b)

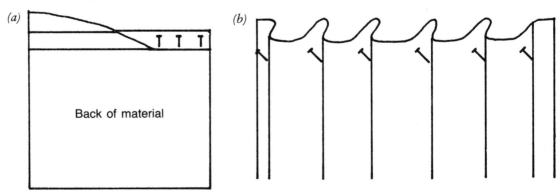

Back of material

Dressmakers' pins can be safely used to attach a number of comparatively heavy items on to pinboard. Paintings on board, or sheets of tin or perspex etc., for display, can safely be held up by carefully angled pins. Single items can be hung on angled pins (Figure 8.14). Pins can be inserted by means of a 'rampin', or 'pinpush' tool, or, in many cases, the use of a strong thimble on the finger is adequate.

Staples are an excellent means of hanging work, but can cause damage if they are driven too far into the pinboard; holding the staple gun at a slight angle ensures that the staple is not driven in too deep, or sellotaping a matchstick under the staple gun vent alleviates the problem. There are a number of tools suitable for removing staples, some are purpose-designed, others less conventional. It is very important to see that all staples are removed cleanly as they can be dangerous to hands if left sticking out of surfaces.

Figure 8.14

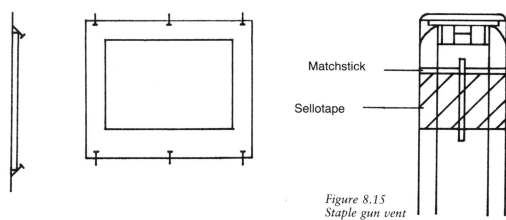

Matchstick

Sellotape

Figure 8.15
Staple gun vent

SIMPLE BOOKMAKING

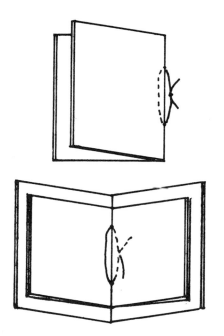

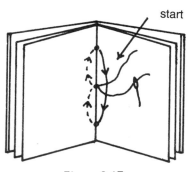

start

Figure 8.17

The challenge to make a book cover which tells us something about the contents is a realistic one for children, and the suggestion of a pattern, collage or montage rather than a pictorial design can lead to some real thinking.

The book can be made, and then filled, or conversely, the contents can be built up (with forethought regarding size and constraints of the method of assembly) and then constructed.

Children enjoy making their own books, and are capable of quite sophisticated techniques by 10 or 11 years of age. Simple techniques can be really effective, and are within most children's capabilities.

The 'card' which requires an outside and an inside page is the first stage, which can be handled by very young children. It can be constructed using a long arm stapler, or by a single stitch and tie of wool or thread (Figure 8.15).

If a cover design or pattern is made prior to the book being constructed, it allows for greater freedom to experiment. The design can be backed on to a stiff lining sheet (sugar paper, or manilla) if necessary. Adhesive need only be spread very thinly *on the surround area* (see Figure 8.16).

Figure 8.16

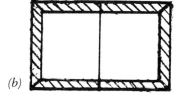

(a)

surround area

(b)

Content sheets should be selected, folded accurately and fixed using a long arm stapler, or by sewing. If the sewing method is to be used, thread and needles will be required. Note the holes made prior to sewing, and the tying off in the centre of the book over the centre thread with a reef knot (Figure 8.17).

If the book is to be put together after the contents are made, a method of dealing with single sheets rather than sections is necessary. Covers can be made in the same way as suggested above, with content paper aligned and placed within.

It must be remembered that there will be loss of working space on the spine side of the book as well as the margin space and children should plan work with this in mind.

Staples, eyelet punch or pliers can be used to fix the pages. Stitching is also possible; it will require an odd number of holes being made, fairly close together, in order to hold the pages firmly. Tie the thread. Finally the pages and covers can be folded back cleanly over a ruler or straight edge (Figure 8.18).

Figure 8.18

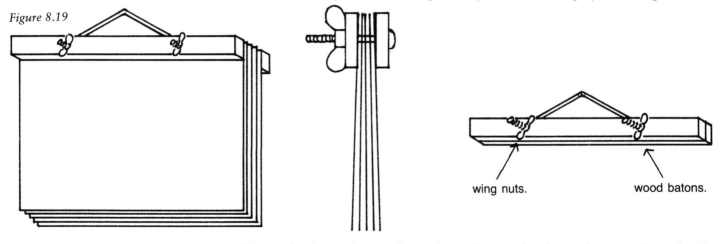

The choice of media used for the cover is very important. Powdery paint or any pigments which rub off or flake are unsuitable and can spoil work. Wax drawings, rubbings, ink flooding, polycell and pigment, or some other adhesives mixed with the colour are appropriate. Paper which distorts when wet will not prove to be a satisfactory finish using this method of bookmaking.

Class books

Class books can be made in the same way as individual books, but on a different scale. However, there are alternatives. The construction of a 'loose leaf' folder which can be used on many occasions is a good way in which to display work (Figure 8.19).

Figure 8.19

Zig zag books made on a base of manilla or other firm substance allows for the work to be free standing, (in which case both sides can be used) (Figure 8.20).

Figure 8.20

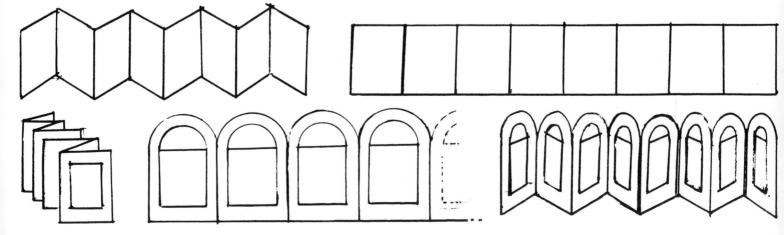

Chapter 9 Handwriting

HANDWRITING HAS been termed 'everyman's craft' and if it is not mastered in the early years, the whole of a child's learning can be impaired. It is of crucial importance that this skill is well taught and that a carefully conceived policy is worked out in each school, taking into consideration (through liaison) the policies of the school the children will go on to.

There has been a good deal of discussion as to the desirability of teaching a style of handwriting. Some teachers deem it appropriate to leave children to their own devices in order to obtain 'writing of character'. While there are no doubt some children who will survive this approach and evolve a good hand, we believe that there are many more whose education is severely marred through lack of guidance.

The teaching of good basic handwriting skills, using a well-shaped simple letter formation, offers good groundwork from which children can develop their own style in later years. Early handwriting skills should lead on to later styles without any necessity for radical change.

Jarman and Bently suggest that handwriting has a threefold function:
- as a tool for clear communications, letters, essays, examinations, etc.,
- as a personal speedy form of note taking, jottings etc.,
- as a calligraphic art form.

In order to fulfil these functions we believe that it is necessary to choose a basic form which can be used as a model throughout the school. This should be of good design, without excessive length in ascenders and descenders; it should lend itself to rhythm and speed quite naturally, to evolve into a cursive (joined) style and it should also be compatible with the printed book form. There are many excellent styles to choose from, some of which are listed at the end of this section. Teachers should be thoroughly experienced in the letter formation of the chosen style and should use it when making teaching aids for the children.

It is important for all members of staff to understand the physical aspects of handwriting in order to help pupils build up good practical ability. Handwriting difficulties arising from incorrect hand position or finger grip, poor posture, inappropriate tools, malformation of letters or sequences often require time-consuming remedial work, yet, with initial care, such problems could have been averted.

It is interesting to note that Margaret Peters considers that a good flowing hand is necessary for children to become confident spellers. There is no doubt that presentation of work does affect assessment and value judgement throughout life, from the need for clear communication of all kinds – letters, essays, and examinations – to day-to-day interpersonal communication. There can be a sense of fulfilment in a well presented piece of work, and children of all abilities can be seen to gain confidence through such achievement. We believe that children should be made aware from early years of the different functions of writing, and that teachers should take these functions into account when evaluating and assessing work.

Her Majesty's Inspectorate in its *Illustrative Survey of 80 First Schools* in 1982 showed some disappointment that there was little evidence that children were helped to produce an individual piece of handwriting that also had aesthetic and decorative value in which they could take pride and from which they could gain satisfaction.

EARLY TEACHING

Some authorities (for example, Rhoda Kellogg and Jacqueline Goodnow) suggest that writing readiness can be ascertained by studying children's scribble and drawing, in terms of manual ability and control, together with shape recognition. It is appropriate, therefore, to see drawing as the best kind of pre-writing activity.

Children should be made aware of good basic letter forms through the teacher's own writing, teaching aids and the model form chosen. *Appropriate tools* will be an important factor and the teacher should observe closely the child's response to different kinds of tool. Pencils, chalks and crayons which make a good, strong, clean mark are useful for beginners; most children find a fairly thick tool easier to handle. There are, however, exceptions, and examples can be found of children responding to a fine, thin tool such as a fibre-tip or biro. Pens can be introduced in drawing activities and many children of eight years and above respond very well to italic pens, or nibs, or chisel-pointed nibs providing they are taught to angle them correctly.

Posture and the height of the writing surface and chair are of the utmost importance, and should be carefully scrutinised by the teacher, who may help the child to experiment with other work positions. The way in which the tool is grasped is also important, as the child may later experience difficulties if the position of the hand inhibits tool usage. Light must be adequate and should fall fully on the work in hand.

Liason with playgroup leaders and parents is important, as they may offer well-meaning but inappropriate guidance if they are unaware of the manner and style in which children will be taught.

Many of the initial activities can involve multi-sensory and creative approaches. Rhythmic patterns – for example those evolved by Marion Richardson – are excellent for building up continuity and flow. Care must be taken to see that they are built up from left to right. It is often useful to challenge children to pattern using the letter forms they need most practice in, taking care to note that the letter formation is correct. All kinds of graphic tools, or a variety of brushes, can be used to make linear interlacing and patterns, which can later be painted, flooded or collaged.

Initially it is important to work individually with the child in order to see that letter formation and left-right sequencing are soundly inculcated. The best way is to sit beside the child, and to work at the same level, guiding his hand, if necessary, to enable him to 'feel' the shape or form a difficult letter. Many children have difficulty in transposing scale when looking at letters and the teacher would do well to use the same tool and letter size as the child when forming letters. Copying and tracing will prove useful, but it is imperative to make quite sure that the child is sequencing from left to right, and forming letters in the correct manner, if future problems are to be avoided. Copying from the blackboard is inappropriate in early years. Transfer of letter shape from a vertical plane some distance away, to a horizontal plane on a worktop, poses real difficulty for many children.

As the child builds up words and rhythm, a natural flow should evolve – as long as an appropriate model of handwriting has been chosen. The development of a cursive (joined) style is normal as the child gains speed and rhythm, and this should be welcomed however early it appears. Children should be encouraged to leave a rhythmic space (approximately the size of a letter o between words): many will space quite naturally. The practice of leaving a finger width between words should not be encouraged as it entails a change of position, and therefore does not facilitate continuous movement. Plain paper will be appropriate for many children, but lined paper, or a grid used underneath bank, bond paper or other writing paper is quite admissible if the child requires it. Very young children are on the whole happier without lines, as it adds a further discipline for them to master, as well as the letter formation, at this stage.

ASSESSMENT AND RECORDING

When considering record keeping in respect of children's handwriting it is desirable to have some form of profile, such as that shown in Figure 9.1, listing basic skills and noting difficulties. These should be laid out in such a way as to point out at a glance the areas in which the child needs further tuition. (Where more than one child shows the same problem, games and challenges can be designed to overcome the difficulty.)

It is useful to keep a piece of the child's writing in order to assess progress or problems at regular intervals. Generally a routine piece of written work will be the most suitable indicator, but there will be occasions when an original item of work can be celebrated and presented by the child. This could be simply written out taking space into account, or decorated and illustrated.

Figure 9.1

HANDWRITING DEVELOPMENT IN THE FIRST YEARS

AIMS: To enable the child to understand the purposes and master the skills of communication through handwriting, and to enjoy the aesthetic qualities of written words.

OBJECTIVES: The child should be able to communicate and express himself in writing with clarity and style.

He should be able to present work in an appropriate manner for the purpose for which it is intended.

He should be experienced in the use of tools and materials, and be able to attain flow and rhythm as well as good letter formation and layout.

SKILLS	TEACHING
Posture	Check height of chair and table/desk/worksurface. Comfortable position, satisfactory light, sufficient working space.
Appropriate tool hold pen/pencil/etc.	Check grip. Firm, relaxed and comfortable - the most usual being between thumb and middle finger supported and steadied by the index finger.
Left to right movement	Plan sequencing challenges. Writing patterns, left to right games, mazes following dots, etc.
Knowledge and discrimination of letters and their formation.	Building up the 'feel' of forming letters, encouraging kinaesthetic enjoyment of shape. Tactile experience with raised letter in textured materials - fur, felt, sandpaper, etc. Letter games and alphabet work. Looking at letters. Imitating, gesticulating, drawing, tracing (in appropriate formation)
	Practising and sorting - families of letters (same heights, shapes, formation, etc). Writing patterns, letter patterns. Ability to discriminate between lower case and capitals (lower case letters enable children to build-up a flow and rhythm, and these should be mastered prior to capital letters being introduced.
Cursive (joined) writing	Drawing experience. Writing patterns - waves, zigzags, loops etc. Introduction of letters into the patterns. Patterns using repeated words, letters, families of letters, groups of letters.
Use of tools	Practice and pattern with a variety of tools including pens with chisel type nib enabling thick and thin strokes to be evolved. Teach the children to angle nibs correctly
	Left handed children. Note problems of positioning, and find appropriate solutions. When children are using pencils and other drawing tools there is little difficulty regarding angle of hold. If however, a thick and thin stroke is required in later stages, there are some excellent pens made for left handers with angled nib units. With a minimum period of individual attention checking angle and hold, these are found to be most successful. [OSMIROID & PLATIGNUM]
Awareness of space and scale.	Practice and play in the use of a variety of graphic tools. Presentation of work in different ways.
	Use of line grids (various) experimenting with margins of surrounding spaces. Discussion.
Aesthetic presentation and design	Opportunity for children to experiment, pattern, and draw with a number of tools, using them to their highest potential. Experience of using a number of surfaces and papers. Encouragement to draft design, plan, and finally present their own work, embellished and decorated if appropriate.

Figure 9.2

Writing position

The writing surface should not be too high - See that the writing arm rests lightly on the table, with the elbow just off the edge.

The writer's head should be kept central (Not sighting along the line).

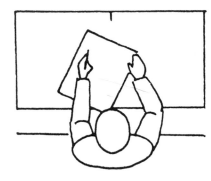

LEFT HAND

RIGHT HAND

Left-hander's requirements:
Paper turned to right.
Pen pointing back at left shoulder.
Right hand moves paper up.
Paper placed left of centre.
View can be improved by holding pen slightly higher up the barrel.

Right-hander's needs:
Slight left-ward tilt on paper.
Pen angle out to right-hand corner of paper (making 45° - 50° angle with writing line).
Left hand moves paper up.

Don't allow this position:

Ensure use of whole hand, avoiding reliance on finger-twisting round the letters.

Letter forms and handwriting can prove to be an excellent project or topic, especially suitable for junior age children. The way in which our alphabet evolved, the history of writing tools, surfaces and materials can be fascinating. Pens can be made from reeds, quills and twigs, and ink manufactured from a variety of sources. Calligraphy through the ages can be studied as a project. The purposes of manuscripts and books can be considered. Manuscripts in reproduction can be introduced, for example, the Book of Kells and other early forms, or illustrated writings and notebooks. Printed letter forms can be researched. Collections of advertisements, posters and prints can be made and shop fronts and street signs studied. Cemeteries often offer interesting lettering and letter forms on headstones. Simple books can be made, written and illustrated, with the covers decorated in keeping with the content.

A number of schools have invited calligraphers to work among the children. These craftsmen and women have been received with great enthusiasm and the real quality of the work can have a profound effect on the children's writing.

Figures 9.2–9.5 offer some suggestions for developing handwriting with children.

Figure 9.3 A basic alphabet:

the quick brown
fox jumps over
the lazy dog

Direction of stroke:

the quick brown
fox jumps over
the lazy dog y k

[tfykx ~ two strokes; i j one stroke + dot
All the others ~ one continuous stroke]

ABCDEFGHIJKL
MNOPQRSTUVW
XYYZ

Note There are some computer programmes showing the formation of letters which can be worked on through the computer itself or by hand. These could well be of use for some pupils, but care should be taken to see that the model chosen bears resemblance to that already being used by the child.

Figure 9.4

Letter families

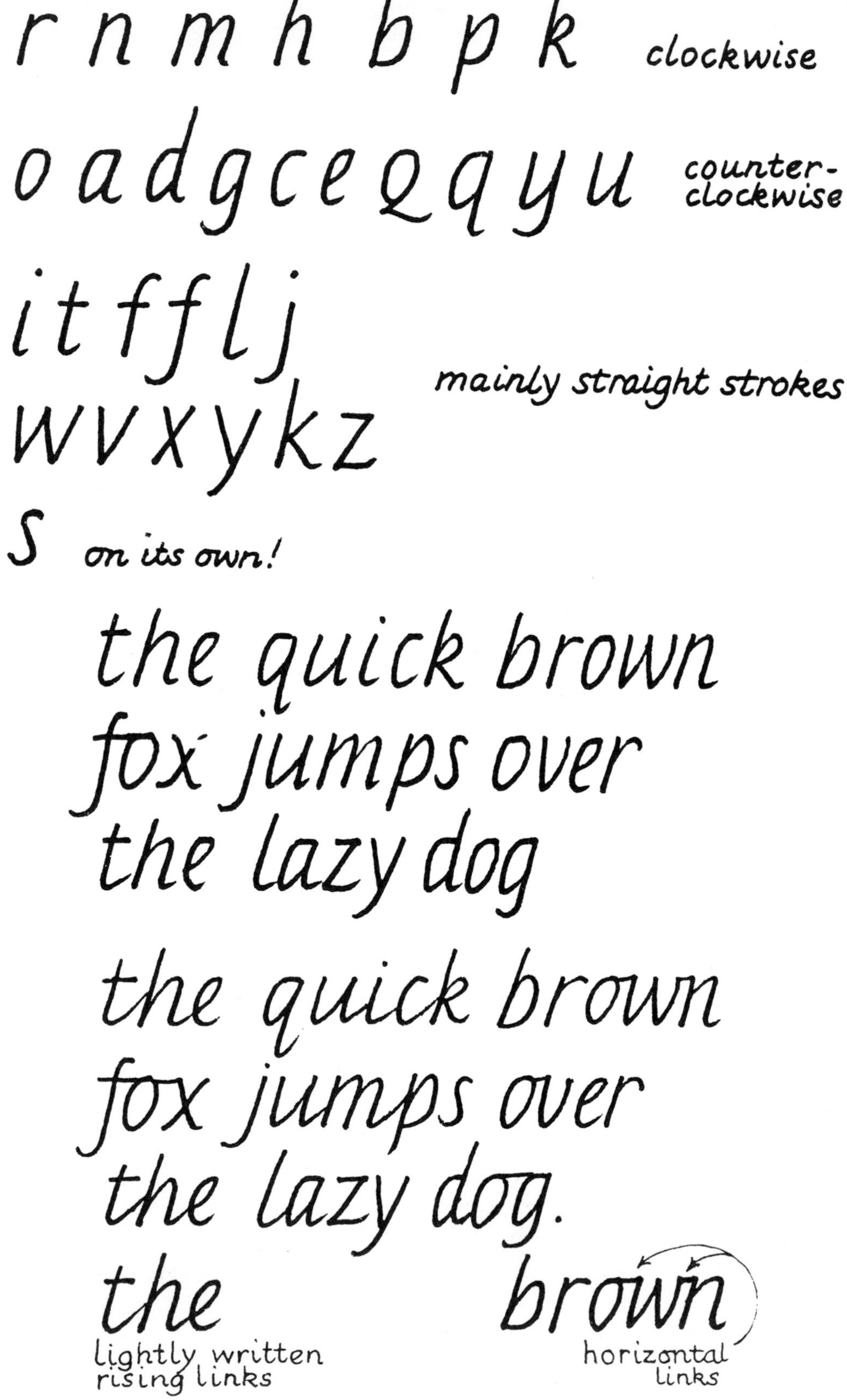

r n m h b p k   *clockwise*

o a d g c e e q y u   *counter-clockwise*

i t f f l j

w v x y k z   *mainly straight strokes*

s   *on its own!*

the quick brown
fox jumps over
the lazy dog

the quick brown
fox jumps over
the lazy dog.
the   brown

lightly written rising links   *horizontal links*

Figure 9.5

ITALIC

Glory be to God for dappled things ~

For skies of couple-colour as a brinded cow;

For rose-moles all in stipple upon trout that swim;

Fresh fire-coal chestnut falls; finches' wings;

Landscape plotted and pieced ~ fold fallow & plough;

And all trades, their gear and tackle and trim.

GMH

Simple ascenders & descenders:

l d b p f

Or written with a flourish:

l d b p f

For special work,
letters may be formed
more perfectly by 'pulling'
all the strokes, e.g.

a s o

Simple Capitals:

A D F

Or Swash Capitals:

A D F

Use sparingly!

Letter height: ⅗ a
Five nib widths
(lower case letters)

Left-hander's
nib and
pen angle.

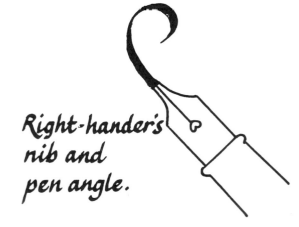

Right-hander's
nib and
pen angle.

RECOMMENDED PUBLISHED
SCHEMES

Beacon Writing Scheme	Fairbanks & Stone	Ginn
Handwriting Activities	Thomas Barnard	Ward Lock Educational
Handwriting Skills	Christopher Jarman	Simon & Schuster Education
Basic Modern Hand	Christopher Jarman	Osmiroid
Handwriting Activities	Thomas Barnard	Ward Lock Educational
Everyday Writing	Ruth Fagg	ULP
I Can Write	Tom Gourdie & Delia Atkinson	Macmillan
The Simple Modern Hand	Tom Gourdie	Collins
New Nelson Handwriting Scheme	Nelson	
Nelson Pre Handwriting	Nelson	
The Irene Wellington copy book	Omnibus Edition	Pentalic/Taplinger (1983)

Wall charts, booklets and guideline sheets are available from Platignum and Osmiroid, including:

PLATIGNUM Italic copy book
Helping (Christopher Jarman, Osmiroid)

23rd January

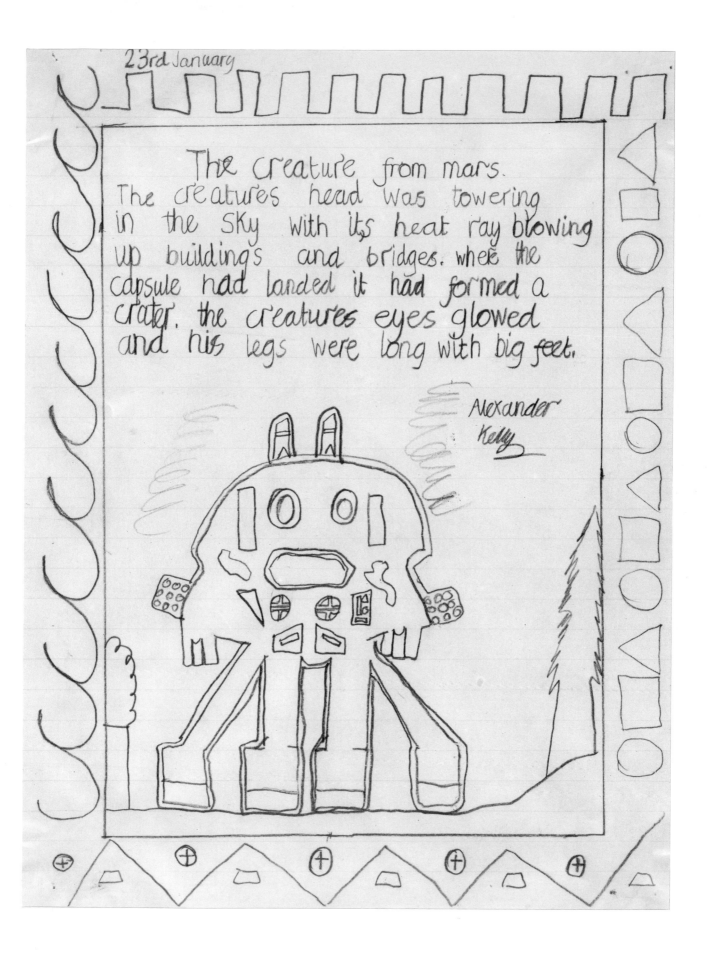

The creature from mars.
The creatures head was towering
in the sky with it,s heat ray blowing
up buildings and bridges. where the
capsule had landed it had formed a
crater. the creatures eyes glowed
and his legs were long with big feet.

Alexander
Kelly

Golden crispy bread poem

Flour Salt yeast Sugar warm water
Then watch the magic work!
Gas bubbles start forming.
The mixture starts frothing.
Until it is ready to mix
with the dough.
When it is thoroughly mixed
we roll and fold roll and fold
until it is ready to
put in the bowl.
Then we leave it.
It starts Swelling
growing Growing Growing
like it is alive.
Then we cut it into fifths
And start shaping it
After we have shaped it

After we have shaped it
we put it on grease proof
paper and glaze it
Then we baked it in the oven
The pale dough.
when it came out it looked all
golden and crispy and tasted
delicous!

Joshua Newman
Class J1B

Chapter 10 Health & Safety Considerations

*M*ANY OF THE Health and Safety requirements in the first years of schooling can be taken care of by a common sense approach and good organisation and 'housekeeping.'

- All schools should keep copies of the most recent directives from the Department of Education and Science in an accessible place in the staff room and all teachers should study them carefully. (*Safety in Practical Studies* HMSO 1982.)
- If the school has a kiln, the publication *Health and Safety in Ceramics* (Pergamon Press, 1987) will be found to be useful.
- All tools and practical equipment should be kept in good condition, stored safely and well organised. Children should be taught the discipline of room and tool management. Appropriate cutting tools should be introduced with care; teachers should be in the room at all times when they are being used.
- Glass containers for water should not be used as this is an unnecessary hazard.
- Floor spillages should be cleared up immediately in order to preclude the risk of children slipping.
- Most pigments and wax crayons are non-toxic, which is a relief for the teacher! Care should be taken when new items are purchased, to see that they are suitable for use with young children.

Health and Safety Inspectors are at pains to point out that the recommendations are to safeguard children being put at unnecessary risk and not to preclude exciting work. It is appropriate for children to be aware of the skills and care needed in working, and be able, through good teaching, to respect tools and materials and handle them safely.

Part Two

Examples of good practice

Scribble based developments (primary school)

All young children scribble, generally they move from this stage when they recognise shapes and symbols within the scribble and sometimes name them. This, together with the characteristics of most older children and adults to 'see pictures' in shapes, damp patches on walls, rocks, or in the fire, led one teacher to experiment in challenging children

a) to scribble

b) to look into the scribble and develop it in some way.

He worked with children of 7–9 years.

The children I was teaching were moving towards the analytical stage of development, and I was aware that some of them were becoming less than satisfied with their own images with their symbolic overtones. Some frustration was apparent, and I was afraid that unless there could be a build up of confidence, and enjoyment of materials (which showed a less vigorous approach to earlier years), they could join the ranks of those who consider themselves 'no good at art'.

In positively challenging children to go back to their familiar scribble I found it possible to build and develop from an area basic to their understanding. The children are at the stage where close observation is highest on the list of priorities, and where better to start from than really looking at their own mark-making?

Scribble, in terms of this experiment, can take a number of forms; including the use of a variety of graphic tools, random print making, (or even squeezing, pushing and pulling clay forms).

The resulting marks were strongly built up and the children encouraged to contemplate in the same way one might view a cloudy sky, or a roaring fire. They were viewed different ways up, at different angles, and from different distances, allowing conscious thought to 'interpret' subconscious or kinaesthetic mark marking.

When a shape, shapes or a suggested form was 'seen' it was then emphasised, reinforced and brought to life by means of a build up of appropriate media. One example began to 'scribble' by painting with the hand and fingers in many different ways, developing it through more printing, painting and using graphic tools. The initial challenge offered an open ended possibility for discovery, with the build up of a number of stages until the work is considered finished.

I have found that building up children's confidence, enjoyment of the subject, understanding of colour, balance and arrangement, together with the potential of the material is a positive and useful teaching strategy for this age group. Scribble is successful because it appears to be 'safe' – it is an area where mistakes cannot be made, where failure is unheard of, where intuitive responses are unfettered, and from where the only way is forward! (See pages 68 and 69, *Pig in a maze*)

Claywork (primary school)

The following accounts describe the responses of two children to stimuli offered at school through visiting puppeteers and a museum expedition.

1 TOTEM POLE POT

The Da Silva puppeteers visited the school and played out the story of a North American Indian boy who was helped by spirits to undertake a number of tasks. The spirits were linked with the totem effigies of the Raven, Bear and other creatures.

A 7 year old girl decided to make a totem pole with heads on it. She considered wood, but rejected it as being 'too hard'. Junk and boxes of various kinds proved to be the wrong shape, so clay was decided upon. It was important to her that the form should be hollow, so she constructed a cylinder; animal heads were modelled separately, then joined on to the tube. After a careful private appraisal she cheerfully announced that she had made a pot.

2 CARAVAN WITHOUT WHEELS

A visit to Stowmarket Rural Museum was organised following a wool project at school. The children were fascinated by a collection of gypsy caravan homes at the Museum.

A 7 year old girl decided to make a model of one of these on her return to school. She decided that a painting would not be satisfactory because she wished to show the outside and the inside, and so chose to model it in clay. She was quite happy with it in spite of totally leaving out the wheels! The main cause for pleasure appeared to be the window shapes she had cut out, thus enabling her to peep inside just as she had at the museum.

Guinea pig project
(middle school:
10–11 years)

This project originally began after I had taken my cat into the classroom for the children to draw. I was anxious to enable them to look very carefully at the cat, the way it was sitting on my lap and how I was holding it, and I therefore talked to them at some length before they began to draw. (The children are in the habit of using a variety of materials and tools, and on this occasion were using chalk, charcoal and black pastel.) See page 49.

Discussion ensued about the cat, and a second one I owned, and the children volunteered information about their own animals. During this conversation some of the children were very keen to bring in their guinea pigs and this was agreed. I felt that the form and shape of the guinea pigs lent themselves ideally for extending experience in clay, and so made the necessary preparation.

Three guinea pigs arrived, and the children were intrigued by differences, albeit slight, between them. We spent time looking at them, as well as hearing about them from their owners. The children gently handled and stroked them, and noticed how their fur grew. Eyes, ears, feet and general shape were also discussed.

I demonstrated how to make pinch pots and join them together to make a hollow shape. (We were using St Thomas's Body, an excellent modelling clay.) The children were already aware of joining techniques for adding appendages. The children began by looking closely at the form of the guinea pig's body. Then they built and joined their pinch pot shapes, and rolled them gently, changing the shape if necessary. [They were encouraged not to make a hole in the form at this stage, as the air is useful in keeping the form full and generous.]

The children often went back to study the animals, particularly when they lacked information about some part of their model. Much problem solving went on as regards appropriate positioning, or ways of adhering details.

I had mixed up red, black and white slips for the children to use, and these were painted on before firing. A hole was made in the body form before the models were finally dry and put into the kiln.

After the first firing some children decided to leave their models at that stage, as they liked the unglazed, comparatively rough-textured finish. Others glazed some parts or covered the surface completely. The choice of glaze available was white opaque, transparent, honey, and black transparent. The children saw examples of

Guinea Pigs. 10–11 years. Ceramic.

these in finished form so that they could make an informed choice. I had also mixed various colours by adding oxides to transparent or opaque white glazes.

The children undertook the glazing themselves using old soft paint brushes, and experimenting with 'dabbing' rather than 'painting'.

The results were diverse and everyone was well satisfied.

Pantomime theme
(middle school:
9 year olds)

The theme of pantomime was adopted for part of the autumn term by the whole school, and was developed in a wide variety of modes and media. A class of nine year olds took the story of Jack and the Beanstalk, and worked from the stimulus of the words and a wide variety of background resources. These included charts and photographs showing castles through the ages, a model castle, books, photographic reproductions, and heraldry showing knights' shields. There were also a number of fairy tale books displaying different kinds of illustration and interpretations of the story.

The aim for part of this theme was to use the impetus and interest generated in the story, and through the resources, to further experience in claywork. It was decided to introduce two stages of practical work, which would enable the children to gain experience of handling clay; and to use clay to build a construction using the slabbing method. The work could develop in a number of ways following this, including language and further art and craft experience.

PRACTICAL WORK 1

Having read and discussed the story the children first considered the character and nature of the giant, and how he would look and behave. The expressions on his face were conjured up and the children looked at one another, miming grotesque effects.

Clay was introduced, and its various properties explored and discussed. Using hands and fingers only, the children were challenged to make models of the giant's head, pinching the features out and pressing and squeezing the round shape. The children rolled the clay into round shapes, and set to work. The heads were then discussed and exploration of the medium through the practical work enabled the children to have a greater understanding of its potential and limitation.

PRACTICAL WORK 2

The children discussed the type of castle the giant would have lived in, and made good use of the resource material. Various aspects were considered including the portcullis, stones, drawbridge, battlements and shields.

Materials

Clay, cardboard, cylinders, modelling tools, rolling pins and guides, oxides and glazes.

A demonstration of slabbing took place. Techniques involved in fitting clay around cardboard cylinders, rolling, pressing, measuring, cutting, joining, reinforcing, and adding decoration by adhering, imprinting and cutting away were introduced.

The children were challenged to build their own castles, and decorate them. Their results were diverse, with little figures climbing up ladders, on balconies, and battlements. Details of windows, doors, drawbridges and buttresses varied.

'Castles'. 9 years. Clay, oxides and transparent glaze.

Techniques used included:

- adding coils – natural forms, decoration and texture.
- adding slabs – doors, windows, stones, flags, shields, portcullis and turrets.
- imprinting – using a variety of formed objects for texturing.
- cutting away – doorways, windows, battlements.
- modelling – figures, trees, weapons.

The children were encouraged at all times to look at their work from all angles, and in different lights.

Decoration

The children were made aware of the characteristics of the oxides, which were mixed with water, and brushed and sponged onto the models. A transparent glaze was added to finalise the effect, and the work was discussed.

(Casting light onto the castles in a darkened room adds a magic which offers splendid opportunities for creative writing stimuli, or for painting.)

A full discussion of the project was undertaken with the children.

Weddings
(primary school:
infant class)

A *Watch* programme on television, showing a Hindu wedding, generated much interest and discussion. An album of wedding photographs was brought to school and more talking ensued. The teacher introduced questions – who had been to a wedding?

'Bride'. Girl. 6 years.
Collage and chalk.
590 × 410 mms.

Had anyone been a bridesmaid? Where were weddings held? Did people wear special clothes? Were there any traditions associated with weddings . . . ? The similarities and differences between an English and the Indian wedding were discussed.

Careful study of the group photographs led to consideration as to who the people were. The bride, bridegroom, best man, the bride's and groom's father and mother were identified. Their clothes, and the colours and materials they chose were discussed.

It was decided that the children would make a group collage, each undertaking one character from an English wedding. First the bit box was replenished, with a variety of materials, textiles and paper, doylies, lace trimmings, tinfoil, etc being included. Then the children drew their chosen characters in chalk on large pieces of sugar paper and built them up in the collage materials, using tearing and cutting techniques. The wedding 'group' was arranged and displayed on the wall, with the titles underneath. Next the children settled to the job of designing, making, and writing the wedding invitations.

This project could have been extended in a number of ways had time allowed, including storytelling, reporting, planning the food for the reception, planning the honeymoon travel, etc.

Inside the human body
(first school
7-year-old class)

The introduction of a turkey bone by a child from an 8-year-old class gave rise to much discussion and speculation, and led eventually to consideration of their own 'inner workings'.

With some confidence the children assured the teacher that they knew what happened inside their own bodies, and it was agreed that they would make drawings to show this. The results were lively and detailed. Some demonstrated a detailed knowledge of the anatomy and inter-relationship of organs and functions, whilst others showed a few symbolic bones and a heart shape.

Girl aged 7 years.

Girl. 7 years.

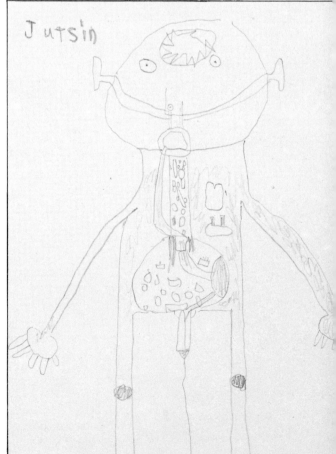

Boy. 7 years.

It was interesting to note that none of the girls showed any sex organs, and that all but one showed an X-ray approach, through their dresses. The exception chose to draw 'Daddy' as she was too shy to undertake herself. He was depicted through his shirt. The boys in the group were not so inhibited and diagrams of all anatomical parts were clearly apparent.

The mother of one small boy called in on the teacher the following day as she was puzzled by her son asserting that he had made a 'dirty drawing' the day before. By the time the teacher had taken the parent to the display of work on the wall, the drawing in question bore the addition of a red crayoned loin cloth!

Old people
(first school:
8-year-old class)

The stimulus for this project was an assembly based on 'families, growth and growing old'. Much discussion followed, with the children contributing thoughts and observations about relatives and old people they knew – their character, how they moved, what kinds of voices they had, the kinds of relationship the children had with them . . .

Practical work took the form of a descriptive portrait of the old person. The resulting 'gallery' of pictures was discussed at the end of the lesson. The children decided that the paintings did not look like old people, and came to the conclusion that the bright pink colours they had all mixed (as usual) for the flesh colours made them look young.

This led to experimental mixing to find colours for skin, resulting in many different shades. The children went on to consider hair shapes, styles and colours; eyes; and the lines and wrinkles caused by different expressions.

Drawing and painting continued, with the children looking at each other, using mirrors and discussing what they saw. Other aspects of the face and characteristics were considered and 'researched'. The children mixed colours for lip hues and freckles, and noticed other shadows and marks.

The project held the children's interest for over two weeks. During this time much oral and written work took place and each child produced a number of 'portraits', often developing and improving them.

Girl. 8 years.

Mrs Keeble
(primary school
5–11 years)

In this small two-teacher school, art is one subject in which all children participate; sharing an experience across the age range, each child interpreting the subject in his own way according to his stage of development.

Art cuts right across our curriculum, finding its way by design or accident into all subjects. It can be a starting point or form a climax to a particular project. Techniques are taught when the need arises and time is spent in looking at and interpreting the things around us and in the rural environment surrounding our school. We participate in village events and many of the villagers are known to us and have become our friends.

None is more so than Mrs Keeble who, for most of her long life, has kept the sweet shop outside the school. The present village children have, like their parents and grandparents before them, bought their sweets from her, enjoying hearing the shrill peal of the bell summoning her from the back parlour, stroking the cat on the chair and choosing their sweets from the wide variety of tall jars displayed in front of them. Her retirement this year was a sad but important event in our lives; one which it was necessary to mark in some way.

It was decided that we should spend a day with Mrs Keeble a week or so after her retirement. This we did. The day was beautifully sunny and we wandered across the road in groups, spending our time exploring the old shop premises and the forge, for the building had once served as a smithy. We looked at pictures and old photographs going back to the turn of the century; we wandered the paths in the old-fashioned

Mrs. Keeble. Powder Colour. Girl. 10 years.

Mrs Keeble

Mrs Keeble is very old and frail
and she's as thin as a nail.
Her body is dainty and her face
is a bit like lace.
She gives us sweets
oh monday we went to meet
her. She was born on 1895
and she likes the bees in the hive.

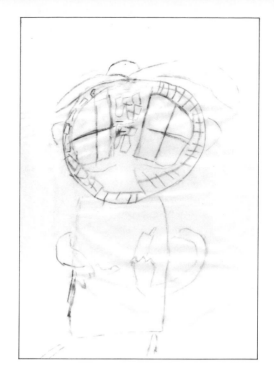
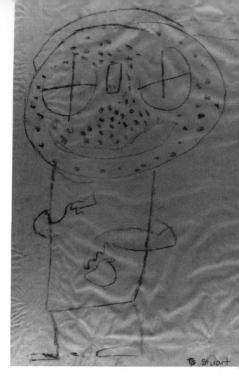

Two drawings by a six year old boy, of the bee keeper who visited the school and put on his hat, masking net and protective clothing.

garden, pinching herbs and smelling their aroma, stroking the old tree planted on Armistice Day 1881. We danced the polka to the music of a crackly record played on an aged gramophone, the older girls wearing Mrs Keeble's old hats. Finally, the whole school drew pictures of Mrs Keeble as she sat under the apple tree, passing round sweets in a large bottle.

Some children later chose to paint pictures and write their thoughts in the form of poems which were displayed at a tea party given for Mrs Keeble and her daughter, Carys, by the infant children who baked cakes and entertained their guests with songs.

The experience has not stopped there – it is on-going. Although we can no longer look forward to purchasing humbugs or liquorice boot laces from her little shop, we can wave to Mrs Keeble from our school garden as she passes by. She and her daughter attended our bonfire party, contributing to our firework fund. We have plans for another visit, this time to see the new room fashioned out of the old shop. Although used by the Keebles, it has taken on the aspect of an informal Museum where mother and daughter relax surrounded by a unique collection of artifacts forming a record of their lives and of a bygone age.

Note We have since invited other people from our village to visit us, including our vicar and a local beekeeper. Our portrait gallery is growing!

Drawing project (primary school 5–11 years)

The following project was undertaken in two classes of a village school. In the first class the children were aged 5 and 6 years, and in the second, 7–11 years.

The purpose of the challenge was to consider the different ways in which the children would respond to a direct visual stimulus following experience which extended the ways in which they used tools. The fact that the children would be at very different stages of development would offer an insight into their individual ways of working. The stimuli offered to the two classes were identical in essence, although the vocabulary used for the introduction differed slightly.

The whole project took place in one morning, with the time divided between the two classes. The children did not see one another's work until later in the day.

Resources Drawing tools, conté crayons – black, white, sepia and ochre – chalk, soft black pencils. Stuffed animals and birds – a rat, a fox, owls and hawks.

PART 1 MEDIA 'GAME'

Each child was given a piece of paper approximately 6″ × 5″ together with the drawing tools. They were challenged to explore the potential of the tools, and in '10 minutes' to cover the paper with every kind of mark they could possibly think of, beginning with one tool to see what marks could be made – thin and thick lines, spots, areas of shading, dark and light shading, overlaying, mixing, rubbing, smudging etc. Other tools could be introduced at any time, and mixing, under- and overlaying built up. The children were encouraged to fill the whole paper until little of the original was left.

The reason for the urgency regarding time, was to generate a 'working approach' and to by-pass possible self-consciousness as to what they were doing.

After a slow start, the children in both classes became engrossed, and enjoyed discussing in the group around the tables at which they were working, the different effects they were getting. The 'results' were highly individual, and in fact had taken nearly 20 minutes for the younger children and 30 minutes for the older class. When the pieces were pinned onto the wall, a lively discussion ensued as to areas and patterns which reminded them of things, and how different they looked when you were further away from them.

*Scribble games.
7–11 years.*

Scribble games. 7 - 11 years.

PART 2

Immediately following this experience, the stuffed birds and animals were introduced, and placed carefully so that each group of children had a clear and unrestricted view of a specimen. The children were excited and a lively conversation ensued as to what the creatures were, where and how they lived, what they ate, together with anecdotes from individuals who had seen, or even kept, animals of the same kind. The older children resorted to books to find out more details of lifestyle, food etc.

Studies of stuffed specimens. 9–11 years. Conté and pencil. (earth colours). There is much controversy regarding the use of stuffed specimens of animals and birds. In our experience children are fascinated and learn much from them. Discussion always takes place in regard to the conservation of wild life. The iniquity of killing creatures in order to preserve their remains always emerges very strongly. Specimens are either historic items or creatures found dead on roads and elsewhere.

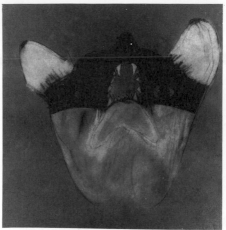

Fox study (from a stuffed specimen). Conté drawing. The nine-year-old girl making this drawing was sitting in a position where it was impossible to see the fox's eyes. She was challenged to draw what she could see. Toward the end of the project she found it necessary to add the eyes!

With everyone settled again around the specimens, and using the same tools they had been experimenting with in the 'game', the teacher introduced visual aspects by 'talking around' the creatures. Characteristics were highlighted in descriptive language, and qualities of beaks, noses, claws, ears, eyes, paws, pattern, texture and shape were discussed.

It was stressed that the drawings were being made in order for the children to find out all they could about the creatures, and that it did not matter if at the end of the morning only a part had been drawn. In the older class it was suggested that they might like to begin with the part of the creature they found most interesting – an eye, or an ear, or a nose perhaps.

In the younger class, following the introduction and discussion, the children chose their paper (from a selection of black, off white, grey and terracotta sugar paper). They quickly settled and went straight to work. Most of the children began with the head shape or the beak, and added body, wings, and legs, followed by a variety of patterning on the body. This ranged from a random filling in of the shape with different patches of coloured conté, to meticulously ordered feather patterns, or organised patterns which had nothing to do with the original stimulus, but were beautifully decorative.

After initially studying the stimulus some children drew without looking again; others looked up from their work on a number of occasions. Some paused to go up to the 'model', looking at it carefully, or gently touching it. Conversation was subdued, and generally about the work in hand. The concentration lasted from 20 minutes to half an hour.

In the older class, the children's concentration was intense, and remained so for over an hour; it could have been extended but for the end of the morning. Those who did finish the drawing were then encouraged to look at a detail or to look from a different angle, or at a different animal. These second drawings were either very much improved on the first, or slighter, depending on a number of factors.

The children worked hard throughout and sometimes commented on things they had not noticed before. Some hardly conversed at all, being deeply involved in their drawings. Most of them were spending as much time in looking as drawing, although some of the younger ones spent long periods drawing, flashing a glance or a long look on occasions.

At the end of the working period most children appeared pleased with their efforts, and commented positively on one another's drawings, noting considered successes in depicting character, details, effects of fur and feathers.

The teacher noted the variety of effects achieved by both age groups through adventurous but controlled use of the tools. She believed that this was a direct benefit from the experimental 'game' challenge prior to the drawing.

Whilst there was a wide variety of responses to this project, with children clearly at different stages of symbolism and analysis, without exception the children were clearly being stretched by the introduction of interesting stimuli. First-hand experience was apparent in all the work, although manifested in very different ways. Some of the older children showed real understanding, and the drawings were of a very high calibre of analysis.

One 11-year-old boy with learning difficulties appeared confused between two specimens he could see, although one was further away from him than the other, a fox and an owl. He made three drawings in succession, each slow and painstaking.

The first, although bearing more characteristics of an owl, with its vertical shape, he firmly called a 'fox'. It had four owl's feet and a tail. The second, again vertical, was also a fox, and had the same characteristics. He was not satisfied with the second, and began a third, which pleased him a little more. The last drawing had some of the characteristics of the first two, but the body was horizontally orientated for the first time.

Note Another possible approach for the experimental period with the older class could have been to introduce the birds and animals at an earlier stage. The challenge could then have been to experiment with the tools to see if the effects of fur, feather and details could be achieved in a number of different ways.

Art and a garden project
(primary school
5–11 years)

In the summer term we started a garden. We obtained a variety of flower and vegetable seeds which included beans, and studied them carefully through magnifying glasses. The children found the shapes and colours fascinating.

During assembly times the whole school studied seeds and drew those selected, much enlarged. Pens, pencils, wax crayons and chalks were used, the latter proving to be the most popular medium. Interesting drawings and designs resulted, some of which were later developed into string blocks and rubbed and printed.

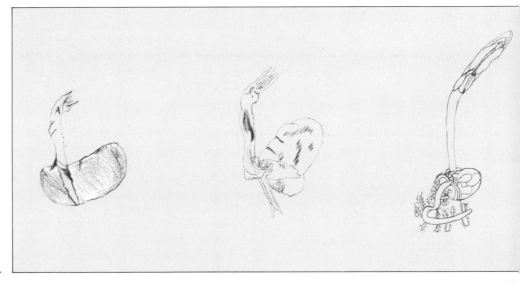

Study of Sprouting Beans. 8–11 years. Pencil.

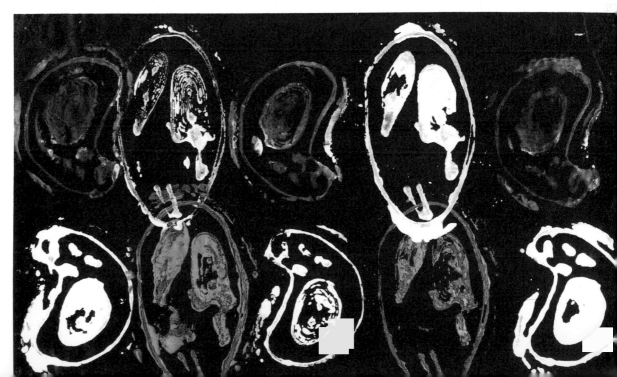

Seed Pattern. 10 years.
String print and paint.
250 × 320 mms.

Further working assemblies found us looking at flowers, at their structure, and the various arrangements of petals, sepals, and leaves, their pattern and colour. Paintings, drawings and collages were made, some showing a searching analytical approach (including some labelling) and often developing into imaginative pictures including landscapes.

Interest built up as the seeds grew and the garden developed. The children spent much time discussing gardens and their many uses. Each child was challenged to design his or her own garden using personally selected media. These pieces of work were fascinating in the way that they gave insight into the child's interests and outlook as well as being a useful diagnostic tool in looking at stages of the children's development, especially regarding spatial concepts.

This final challenge, in the case of the infant group, was combined with a garden diary, and terminated a project which had involved nearly every aspect of the primary school curriculum.

Tortoise project
(town middle school)

This project was designed to heighten observation, and build up experience of the basic elements of art – line, shape, tone, colour, pattern, texture and form, using a variety of materials and techniques.

Tortoises were chosen as a subject of interest for the children in the hopes that they would engender curiosity and heighten perception.

The children were encouraged to bring in their own tortoises as well as those kindly lent by other children and members of staff. It was necessary to make safe tray arrangements with sides, in order to stop the creatures from falling off the edge of tables and desks.

STAGE 1

Materials and equipment

Drawing paper (various) graphite sticks, pencils.

Challenge

Much time was spent in discussing the variety of patterns, shapes, lines, etc, on the tortoises. A bank of words was built up, to describe various characteristics observed. The texture of the neck and head, the size of the eyes, and shapes and patterns on the shells were all commented on, and gently touched and felt.

The children were divided into groups with a tortoise on each table, safely penned into its sided tray.

The children were challenged to make experimental marks with their pencils to represent any of the details found on the tortoise. Following the exploration they were asked to record the shapes, patterns and lines they observed from their particular viewpoint.

STAGE 2

Materials and equipment

Potatoes, knives, ready-mixed powder paint, newspaper, sugar paper, flat tiles and rollers and protective overalls.

Challenge

The children were asked to select some patterns from the previous drawings and to translate them into a potato print. Each potato had a number of prints cut into the half section and sides. A study of the tortoise was built up on the papers. Some children experimented with collaged newspaper and print.

The class divided into groups following the different challenges which they had evolved.

STAGE 3a

Materials and equipment

Adhesives and glue sticks, coloured papers and boards.

Challenge

The papers and boards were explored to achieve different textured qualities by tearing, folding, squashing, cutting and rolling.

Following consideration of a colour scheme for the tortoise, designs were built up from earlier studies, and carried out in vigorous collage.

Tortoises'. 10–11 years.
Pencil, and wool collage.
Boy 11 years. 400 × 450 mms.

STAGE 3b

Materials and equipment	A selection of white card of varying thicknesses, scissors, adhesives, etc.
Challenge	Following experiment with the card, building it up into relief in a variety of ways, the children referred to their earlier work and built up a tortoise with special consideration for shape and pattern.

STAGE 4 GROUP ACTIVITY

Materials and equipment	Wire and wirecutters, fabrics, paper, polystyrene sheets and blocks.
Challenge	The children were given the task of using the wire in a variety of ways, bending, wrapping it with other materials and fixing the ends into the polystyrene to build up patterns based on earlier drawings.

(The original idea for this activity followed discussion of a wall hanging which had been introduced into the school from the 'loan scheme'. This consisted of a series of wrapped fibres arranged in an abstract pattern by Margot Barrow.)

Other possibilities which could be considered: tortoise collage using stitchery and fabrics, string or woven threads; direct three dimensional modelling in clay; researching form, shape, pattern and texture.

Note A later project was undertaken when the teacher borrowed a number of baby rabbits. The children worked directly into clay, having discussed and gently handled the animals.

Sky (primary school 7–11 year old class)

We began by going outside to look at the sky and then looked at a variety of pictures of skies. We talked about the effect of time of day, seasons and weather. After this, the class experimented with mixing paints to get various shades of one colour. During the next few days we watched the sky. We were lucky enough to get a great variety of skies and spectacular sunsets. In the next session, each of the children painted many examples of skies seen. They were encouraged to mix shades of colour. After a lengthy discussion of suitable words, they wrote prose passages or poetry about skies and clouds. These were some of the descriptive words the children used:

> 'Clouds move and swirl.'
> 'They are towering on stormy days.'
> 'Clouds can be fluffy, puffy, fat and white.'
> 'When the sun shines on a cloud, one side is grey and dull and the other side is bright.'
> 'In summer the sky is blue but when it is stormy the sky is grey and the clouds look cold.'
> 'Clouds are made of water. If it is rainy and sunny there is a rainbow in the sky.'
> 'They look like cotton wool and sometimes like ice cream in a cone.'
> 'Sunset is at the end of the day and there are the oranges, reds, yellows and purples.'
> 'Sometimes the clouds are woolly like a beard.'
> 'Today the sky is blue and the clouds are fluffy and whispery.'
> 'When the sky is misty and foggy the clouds disappear.'

Discussion of the paintings led to some interesting considerations of the effects and qualities of paint, and colour mixing.

Art and language development providing mutual stimuli (primary school)

We decided to introduce our new reading scheme to the parents as part of a Language Development Exhibition. There is nothing so effective as a deadline to provide impetus and, as the school places strong emphasis on art based work, it was a natural progression to combine language with art to provide mutual stimuli.

To this effect, in order to motivate the class, James Reeves's poem *The Hippocrump* was read and discussed with the children, then built upon to create mental images of similar beasts – using words to stir the individual child's emotions, gradually gaining momentum until each experienced an explosion of feeling through the chosen medium.

'*Close your eyes and imagine that you are being chased by a Hippocrump ... to escape you go into a gloomy shed ... is the Hippocrump outside? ... you stretch on tiptoe to look through the cob-webbed window ... and there is the Hippocrump staring back in at you ... you are nose to nose with a Hippocrump! Open your eyes and paint what you saw in your imagination.*'

The procedure was then reversed. Teachers selected eight Hippocrump paintings which they felt would provoke animated conversation. The pictures were numbered and displayed for the first time in another classroom. The teacher, aiming to promote richness and quality in language, asked

'*Where do you think these monsters live? ... What do you think they eat? ... What do you think they do? ... Are they kind or cruel? ... Can you think of a name for one of the monsters?*' After allowing time for thinking and discussion the children

Miss Cat Crip Cobble has a very funny hat. She has long water reeds in her hat and she gives them water every day. This is very funny because she has a bit of the sun in her hat. When the water reeds die, she goes to the river and gets some more. When she waters them she has to be very careful not to water the sun. She has the job of Police Inspector. She wears normal clothing although she is an inspector. This is because she still has the sun in her hat.

Description by a girl aged 9 years.

Miss Cat Crip Cobble. Boy. 9 years.

'repainted' the visual images with words. The results varied from journalese style headlines backed by 'on the spot reports' to long, flowing prose and succinct poetry.

This work was followed up with children writing poetry and prose inspired by 'scribble pictures' and portraits from written character descriptions initiated by a visiting author. Our Language Development Exhibition became so interrelated and involved with art that each became an extension of the other.

Higgly Haggly Hiawatha is an Indian who unlike the other Indians always has his clothes hanging out. He has the only shirt in the tribe and he does look funny:

'In the eighteenth century the Sioux tribe were going to war, but on Planet Zepton there is another war going on between Planet Zepton and Pluto. The Zepton's queen thought she would get help, so she sent a spaceship down to Earth. Meanwhile on Earth the Sioux were fighting the cavalry. Suddenly the spaceship came into sight. There was a dazzling white light when it stopped. There were no Sioux left. They were all in the spaceship. When the spaceship got back to Planet Zepton the Sioux were transformed into Zepton warriors. They were given laser guns. The Chief of the Sioux tribe is Higgly Haggly Hiawatha and the Queen's name is Mrs Mary Wild and Hairy. Those two were in charge of the army. The battle began. The Zepton troops set off on Pluto to attack the Plutonions, but the Plutonian troops were fully prepared for the Zepton troops. The Plutonian men were better equipped than the Zepton troops and the Plutonians had more men. When the battle began there were zips, zaps, bangs, pings, pongs, tips, taps and lot of other funny noises. Then the Plutonian king fell. The king was dead. Then the Zepton troops captured a Plutonian guard and forced him to tell him to tell them the name of the king. He said, 'Queeny monster.' then the troops went back to Zepton.'

Story by a boy aged 9 years.

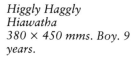

Higgly Haggly Hiawatha 380 × 450 mms. Boy. 9 years.

Display: trees
(first school)

[Written by the member of staff responsible for display and visual environment.]

A colleague worked for a term on a project on trees – their growth and environment. In order to extend the project further it was decided to move some of her class work to the library area. In consequence, I was asked to make trees and wood the subject of my display area in the main foyer.

The project leader had borrowed numerous samples of wood and bark from loan collections. I used these together with a large colour poster depicting the most commonly known trees of the British Isles. The poster was one of many things brought to me by the children. It belonged to a six year old girl who had been given it as a present. She was delighted to see it given pride of place on the display.

At the start of setting up a display I inform each class and ask for anything that they have at home which might be suitable. Usually I specify the things that I most require, but not too rigidly as this might inhibit the children. I do like to have as great a variety of items as possible!

In this instance I asked the children for anything wooden – dolls; toys; ornaments; kitchen, workshop or garden tools, either in polished or natural form; interesting pieces of wood, bark etc. I was brought such a vast amount of lovely and interesting items that I was obliged to exchange some so that all could be shown at some time during the duration of the display.

Items were grouped appropriately. Unpolished beech items were displayed together, eg kitchen tools, small toys, etc., as were the polished wooden items, eg plates, bowls, ornaments and boxes. As far as possible each type of wood was identified and the item labelled.

A parent brought me two lovely wooden painted puppets which were a colourful addition to the display. These were noticed, unwanted, at a jumble sale and had been rescued specifically for my display. These were grouped with other brightly painted ornaments, eg a fishing boat and a cockerel from Portugal.

The very small items like pencil sharpeners, pencil ends and miniature trains were also grouped together.

The children in my class studied pictures of trees and discussed the trees in their own gardens as well as trees seen in the parks and open country. They were encouraged to look very carefully at them when they saw them again. They painted their favourites and the cherry-tree was easily the most popular, being painted in blossom and in fruit. I arranged these along the lower front of the display. Pine trees, sycamore and willow were also chosen by the children as favourites.

The centre area and the display was occupied by a fine photograph of a woodland scene which had been in the staffroom but was loaned for the occasion.

I found a delightful poem called *The Seed* by Aileen Fisher which I wrote out in large print and illustrated with drawings and with real seeds.

Upon the nearby windowsill I set out some small doll's furniture including a set of chairs from Cyprus, and an impressive set of child's furniture, a sideboard, a refectory table and a bench seat, which were made in imitation mahogany.

Children always respond to a display if they have contributed to it and if the subject is one that interests them. They will firstly come to see what has been done with their contribution and will then look at everything else. This leads to great discussions among groups of children who then look at what others have brought and at the other parts of the display, information and books etc.

Children will look while passing and will suddenly realise that they have something at home which could be relevant to the display, and bring it to me next day.

Whilst looking and discussing, children inevitably come to the poem or piece of prose which I try to include, and will read it out loud together and to each other. It is especially enjoyed if it is something they know or recognise. Members of staff will very often use displays to further their own classroom work, and it is possible for the idea to develop and change as time goes on. Items are changed for others, and children's work can be incorporated. It can be seen as a stimulus to conversation, vocabulary, writing, all forms of art and craft, and an extension of knowledge and experience regarding the nature and quality of the items.

So, although a display is primarily a visual thing, its impact on the school can be very far reaching if the subject chosen has been an appropriate choice.

Some examples of school displays.

'Tools', 'Shiny things', 'Round things', 'Texture table', 'Fur and Feathers', 'Individual colours – Red, Green, Blue, etc – Black, White, Silver, Grey, etc', 'Long and Thin', 'Pattern', 'Stone', 'Wood', 'Wool', 'Dappled things', 'Holes', 'Spring', 'Autumn', 'Tiny things', 'Boxes', 'Toys', 'Reflections', 'Stripes', 'Spots', 'Roots' . . .

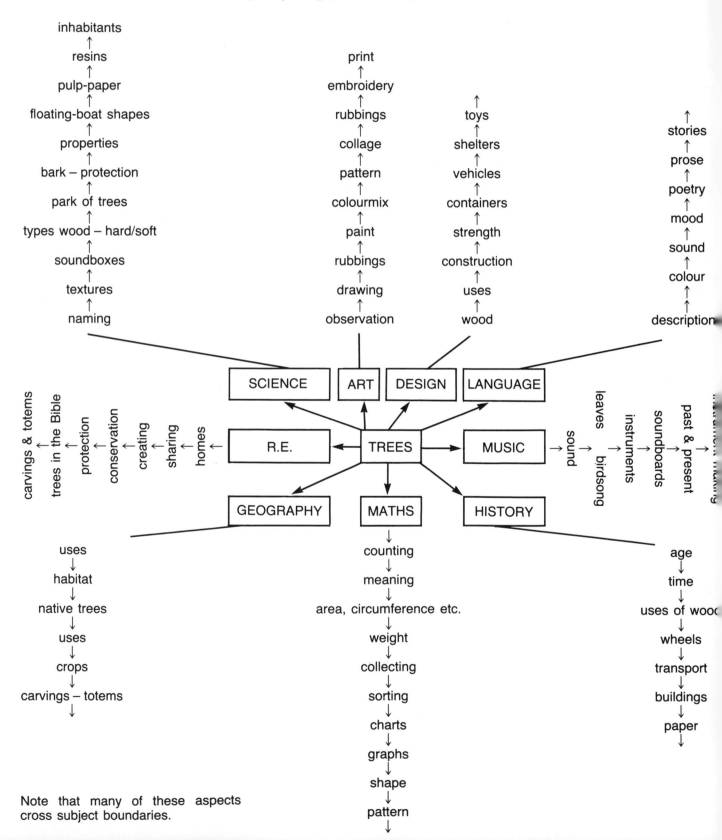

Note that many of these aspects cross subject boundaries.

Woodpecker. Boy. 5 years. Paint: (black, red and grey). 450 × 240 mms.

Group work – 'The Snowman' (A painting by six children, 9–11 years)

The Christmas theme for our hall was to be 'snow', a very simple, ordinary subject for the festive season! This unanimous decision was taken with the idea that it would give all children plenty of scope to produce snowy pictures, patterns, models and designs as creatively as they could. We were determined that the walls, ceilings and every spare corner would vibrate with the children's snowy creations.

Needless to say, many children's minds turn to snowmen when given the wide subject of snow and we were inundated with whole families of snow people. The children, throughout the school, were not directed in the way these should be produced and we were not disappointed with the results. Snowmen of all kinds, shapes, sizes and nationalities appeared day by day. Many by the younger children (five, six and seven year olds) were drawn in paint on large sheets of paper and decorated and clothed in a variety of ways. Large snow ladies with gold ear-rings, pearls, wigs; sophisticated members of the snowman family in pen and ink, collage, paint, crayon and felt pen, all with their own personality and character, emerged from the Middle and Upper Junior Department. Every one of our 290 children depicted his or her own idea of a snowperson and these were displayed all over our main hall on a background of textured snow. A small group of children had thoroughly enjoyed painting this with spray guns, aerosol, sponges, hands, large brushes, rollers, and many other implements to achieve the cold feeling of snow falling, drifting and settling on earth.

Beforehand, and while the children were deeply involved in their snowmen, language in all its various forms helped to fire their imaginations. One seasonal book, which is always guaranteed to be a firm favourite with children, is Raymond Briggs' *The Snowman*, a beautiful story in delightful illustrations, full of winter feeling, which can be used in numerous ways with children as a springboard for learning.

This story provided the subject for a giant picture which, it was decided, would be the focal point in our main hall.

The picture was to be tackled by a group of six children, from nine to 11 years. We particularly wanted the children to work together without direction from staff or parents in the school. In doing so, this would really challenge the children to talk, listen, discuss, observe, be aware of each other's work and problem solving in order to achieve the results that they wanted and would accept.

To help the children achieve some continuity they were given as much time to work together as the timetable would allow at this busy time of the year. Firstly, it involved much discussion about the materials that they were going to use, the part of the story they wanted to share with others or the part that inspired them to want to be creative and the feelings in the story which they wanted to communicate. At this stage, they were encouraged to look at the book of *The Snowman*. They were strongly urged to allow themselves to be influenced by the colours, feelings and techniques, but advised not to copy the illustrations and subject matter.

It was interesting to stand on the sidelines, watching and listening without inhibiting the children's freedom. It took the group almost a whole school day to decide what they were actually going to portray and who in the group was going to tackle particular parts of this enormous work. The children knew well who had certain strengths and weaknesses within the group but they were very modest and tactful with each other in the early stages. They appeared to be quite fair, democratic and reasonable. There was no emergence of a group leader until half way through the project, on day 3. The children allocated each other certain areas of the picture and after they had made a start planning out their particular section they had to be reminded, as a group, to stand back every so often, and view their work. At times, they were quite content to work on their piece without considering each others' progress and results. Gradually they learned that this was a vital key to the success of the picture and, as they became more used to doing this, more heated discussion, arguments and firm decision making took place!

The length of time involved in producing the picture was approximately one week (5 days), rather than one day a week for five weeks. It was felt that as this was a new way of working for the group, continuity was important. Concentrated working over a shorter period of time made sure that the children would remember designs and

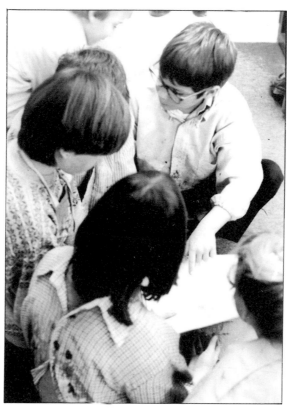

plans which had been made and their imaginations would be more likely to remain fired over a few days rather than over a few weeks, especially as they were working on their own.

It was pleasing to see the children using techniques, methods and skills that they had previously learned, in a creative and sensitive way. Considerable thought was given to the coldness they wanted to portray through colour, texture and shape. The background and foreground were fairly vast areas, but each member of the group strictly adhered to his or her own area – each child mixing their own colour and blending and matching their piece to correspond with everyone else's work.

The painting was pronounced finished after one school week and the group were pleased with their results. Evaluating their work, the children themselves thought that more of the story could have been portrayed. However, they did remark that in doing so, they would have destroyed the cold, mysterious emptiness that they wanted to transmit to the onlooker. Towards the end, they all agreed, they had hurried instead of working on the more detailed pieces slowly and carefully. Much of this was probably due to the immaturity of the group and the knowledge that Christmas was not far away – in some ways they were working to a deadline. They all said they would like to work again in this way, providing they could choose the group!

Shelter project
(10 year old children)

This project was linked to the humanities curriculum, and comprised one term's work. First the idea of the need for shelter for human beings and animals was considered and discussed. Then the project developed as follows:

1 Taking a large collection of basic materials which included small pieces of stone, twigs, wood, raffia, dried grass and clay, the children were challenged to construct shelters for two-inch figures. The shelters were then evaluated in terms of their varying qualities, ability to withstand weather, etc; improvements and developments were considered.

Drawings and paintings of these shelters were made. Some were brought to life by indications of climatic conditions, and the sort of people living in them. Others took the form of descriptive drawings of how they were constructed. Plans were also drawn.

2 Plans were made of their own homes, showing their own rooms in detail. Children were also asked to imagine that a huge saw had cut the building in two, and to draw what they might see in one half. Looking at elevations in architects' drawings enriched this experience.

3 The children collected pictures from magazines and supplements at home and in school, of windows, doors, brick and other building material patterns.

Drawings of apertures and surface pattern were made from their own homes and the school buildings.

4 A visit to a building site was arranged. Special attention was paid to the construction of the building materials and tools used and men and machines at work. The sounds and smells of the site were also highlighted. Notes and drawings were made. Back in the classroom the children explored with powder paint, card, sponges, brushes, graphic tools and rubbings to find building material and surface patterns to be used in representing houses.

5 Groups of children were given large quantities of newspaper, adhesive, wool and string and challenged to construct a shelter large enough for one person, and strong enough to get inside and sleep in. When it was realised that tightly rolled newspaper was a very strong material, various ways of construction were employed.

6 Research into the ways in which living things build, grow or find shelter led to drawings, paintings and textile experience. Shells were studied, as well as plants being sheltered by walls in the school grounds.

Drawings and recording of colour led to the construction of a wall, with the children as a group using their own initiative to make texture bricks using sponge, foam and matchboxes covered with a variety of materials including nylon tights.

The form and shapes of plants, with special consideration of how they grew were interpreted in paper fabrics, wire and pipe cleaners.

7 Abstract concepts of the idea of shelter were discussed, (for example, the idea of a family providing shelter for a baby or child, as it offers protection etc.)

A variety of 'family', or parent and child pictures and reproductions were introduced for discussion.

Nativity themes proved a seasonal asset, and a design was developed for a window for the Christmas decoration.

Other work out of school included the selection of a favourite building, and taking into consideration the way in which you would describe it if you were an estate agent and were commissioned to sell it. [Through pictures as well as the written word.]

Raft project
(primary school 10 and 11 year old class)

This project began with a discussion of rafts, their purposes, and the variety of things they were made from. I challenged the children, if they were interested, to build models at home, and motivated them as strongly as I could.

In different circumstances this project could have taken place at school, but there were limitations at the time regarding space, materials and tools.

The children were used to thinking for themselves, and had had a wide experience in school of building and making things. The briefing was simple. 'A model raft that would float'.

About two thirds of the class produced a raft; some were made entirely by the children, some had contributions from parents.

A wide variety of scrap materials was included: planks of wood, hardboard, chipboard, garden rubbish, lolly sticks, drinking straws, polystyrene, cotton, fabric, plastic, string, nylon thread, paper and card.

The rafts were sailed on the swimming pool. All of them floated, but some proved to be too light and blew about in a manner which would have endangered the life of the mariner. These we decided were not really successful. (These were made from the plastic straws stuck together.)

All the rafts had square sails and only travelled in one direction, and lively discussion ensued to see a way to remedy this. One line of enquiry was into the way in which yachts with triangular sails manage to sail into the wind.

One of the rafts had a rudder which could be set at different angles, but this did not seem to make any difference to the direction of the sail. Another one was very well made out of bamboo logs tied together, but it kept blowing over. Taking experience from the Kontiki expedition, we pushed a stabilizer down between the logs. This, in turn led to 'investigation of various kinds of stabilizer'!

A school visit was arranged to see an exhibition of barges with flat bottoms and leeboards, following which some of the children built model yachts from balsa wood which proved to need outriggers to stabililze them.

Returning to our rafts, we tried to test them by putting weights on them until the point of sinking. This led to a discussion of the dangers of shifting loads and of the origin of the original and modern Plimsoll lines. Blocks of wood of different types were weighed and placed in water to see how far down in the water they went (one block actually sank). This was repeated in salt water and a number of experiments were carried out so that the children could observe the buoyancy of water.

The mother of one child told me that her daughter and a friend had constructed their raft unaided out of garden twigs which they had painstakingly stuck together: Unfortunately, when it was placed in water in the bath, it fell apart, and the youngsters had shown considerable determination in starting again with a non water-based glue.

The project continued to develop, and the rafts were set into a jungle background, using coloured papers and paint. Stories were written about jungle 'plane crashes and escape by raft'. Drawings and paintings were made of the models, and of the models in their setting, as well as of the barges on the barge visit.

Reference books proved useful throughout, and were used to find out about different types of boats. We were very interested in finding out about a ship of the future . . . with sails!

Note This project, undertaken in part out of school, worked well mainly because of the initiative and experience which had been engendered in school.

Church project
(primary school 8–11 years)

This project was undertaken by a class of eight to 11-year-olds, working with help, guidance and minimal direction from a group of parents, the Rector and the Headmaster. The adults were fully aware of their roles as initial consultants, but not leaders.

The project centred on studies of the local church. A very broad outline was agreed by the adults, who also considered possible sources for further information.

Resources
Visits to the church. Books, photographs,
experience of local craftsmen, etc.

The pupils were introduced to the project, and ideas for development and any foreseen problems were discussed. Large wall hangings were envisaged, together with models, prints, drawings, paintings and written matter. The initial planning allowed for the children's own initiative to flourish, and the adults were flexible enough to encourage and accept the children's ideas and solutions to problems. Direct help was only given on requests for information or in choosing suitable adhesives, and on occasion, raw materials.

Close observation was the key to the work, and much time was spent in studying the church at first hand. Pupils drew, measured, noted and experimented until they were satisfied that they could add to some aspect of the work in hand. Where possible the adults extended the children's experience – for example, a stonemason provided technical information on building.

The children had envisaged what they were aiming to do and often sketched their experience and techniques in order to achieve their aims. Planning, designing, and carrying out those designs were part and parcel of the ongoing work. Every pupil participated and was represented by some part of the work they finally presented and displayed.

The initial wall hanging was the forerunner of a series which, when taken together present a view of the village community as a whole. Houses, farms, hedgerows, trees, ponds, and the river have all provided fruitful challenges to further the children's education.

Notes on 'Bigod's Suffolk 1173' History/Drama/Art/Craft/Design

Art and Design work which involves in part the discovery and experience of processes, techniques and the use of different materials can offer substantial opportunities for cross-curriculum work.

In these photographs, primary children are working at Orford Castle. They are taking part in a project called 'Bigod's Suffolk 1173'. For a day, they are in role as apprentices recruited by the Constable to help with building work on the castle. The emphasis is upon 'learning by doing'. As far as possible they are working with the materials and equipment which would have been in use during the 12th century. Some cook on open fires, others build walls with the stone mason, make and fire shafts with the bowman, while more tend animals – sixteen different activities in all.

In doing so, they are not only discovering through experience how things would have been done in the past, but they are also learning techniques of the present. In the illustrations, history, drama and environmental science unite in a common aim, to help children not only to learn about, but also to understand the past. The day spent at Orford is part of a longer period of classroom study which involves research, discussion, written and practical work on the Normans.

Apprentices try making coloured inks using a variety of material – soot, egg yolk, leaves and natural dyes. Later they will sharpen goose feathers into quills and try writing on parchment.

Under the supervision of the Mantler, willow saplings are stripped, the bark woven into belts and shoes, while the supple wood is used for baskets and mantlets (shields for the bowman).

Wool is clipped from the sheep. Later it will be carded and spun by the children.

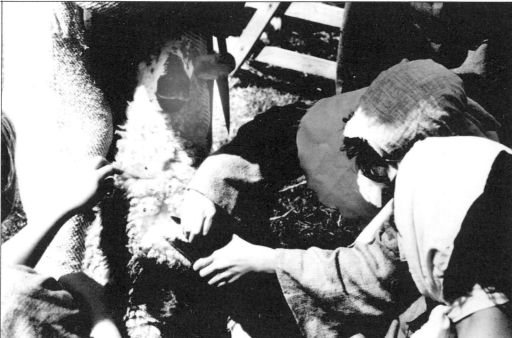

Over open fires, skeins of wool are dyed, using natural materials gathered from the surrounding countryside – blackberry leaves, elder, walnut. The dyed wool will pass to the Wardrobe where other groups of children will weave it into cloth or stitch it into tapestry.

Topic – a medieval 'Pot Pourri'

This was a Christmas entertainment developed from the main topic on Castles for children of 5–11+)

OBJECTIVES

a To use drama, language and music to recreate the type of entertainment which would have been held in the Great Hall of a castle at Christmas.

b Through linking Art and Craft activities to provide the children with a variety of experiences which would ultimately give flavour and visual impact to the production.

Method: The topic developed in several stages; teachers, parents and children working as a team, developing ideas so that each component interacted with the others.

STAGE 1

Great Hall of a castle
Resources: Photographs, slides, books.
Visit: Framlingham Castle.
Discussion: 'How could we give the classroom the appearance of the Great Hall of a castle and in so doing set the scene for our entertainment.'
Activities: Building up a large floor diagram with the children and parents which led on to practical work.

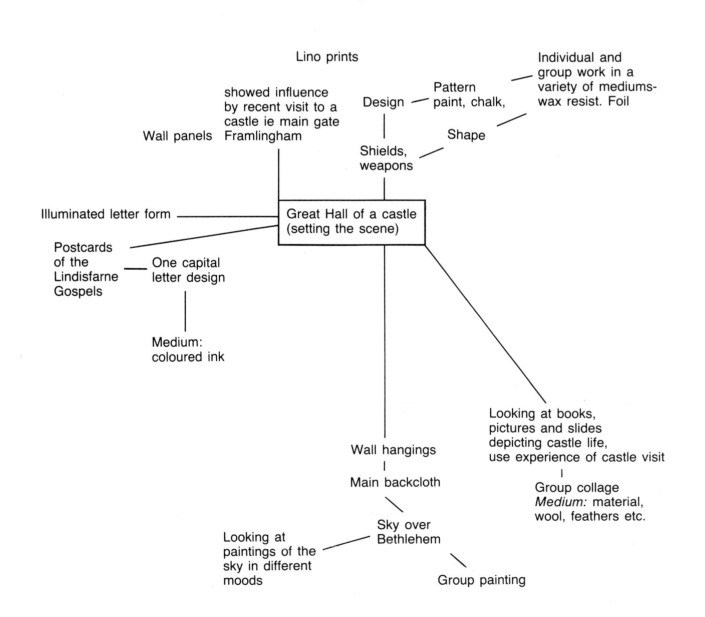

STAGE 2

Following discussion and work on drama, language and musical activities, art and craft sessions concentrated on linking with these.

Activities – grouped

a Minstrels' costumes/Pages' costumes
   Discussion and challenge: The children had to design a simple tunic shape with suitable decoration.
   Results: Hessian tunic, decorated with wool and an appliqué shield motif in felt.

b Recorder cases
   Discussion and challenge: To design a recorder case with suitable decoration.
   Results: Felt cases with an appliqué motif.

c Animal masks
   [To be used in the story of Chanticleer and Pertelote and a special Bear Mask for the Bear and Trainer Act]
   Resources: books, pictures, studying farmyard animals
   Results: Masks worked in sugar paper, card and decorated with paint, tissue paper, etc.

d Rod puppets
   Discussion and challenge: Making rod puppets (sturdy twigs and stockinette construction). Designing and making characters in the play.
   Activities:
   ● Constructing puppets, adding individual features and effects using material scraps, wool raffia etc;
   ● Designing and making costumes.
   ● Working as a group to produce the large dragon puppet. Paper plates decorated with coloured paper, painted, melted wax crayons and suspended from a length of dowel.

e Puppet theatre
   Discussion and challenge: To design a puppet theatre with sufficient height to hide the puppeteers, it had to be sturdy but manoeuverable; decorated to enhance the impact of the play [it would be necessary to carry it on and set it up in the great hall, as part of the performance].
   Activities: After much experimentation we used three panels of the Wendy House decorated with hand pattern and oil crayon portraits of the puppets.

STAGE 3

Incidentals and effects
Discussion and challenge: What effects would give the 'Pot Pourri' more authenticity?

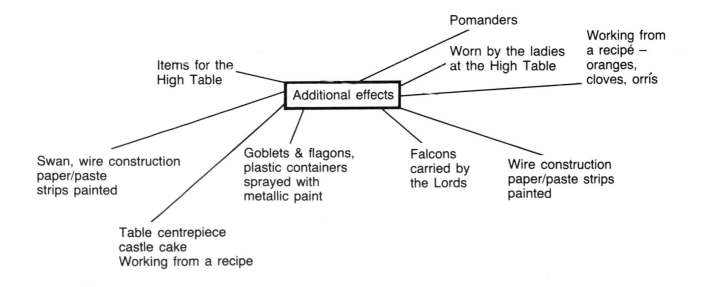

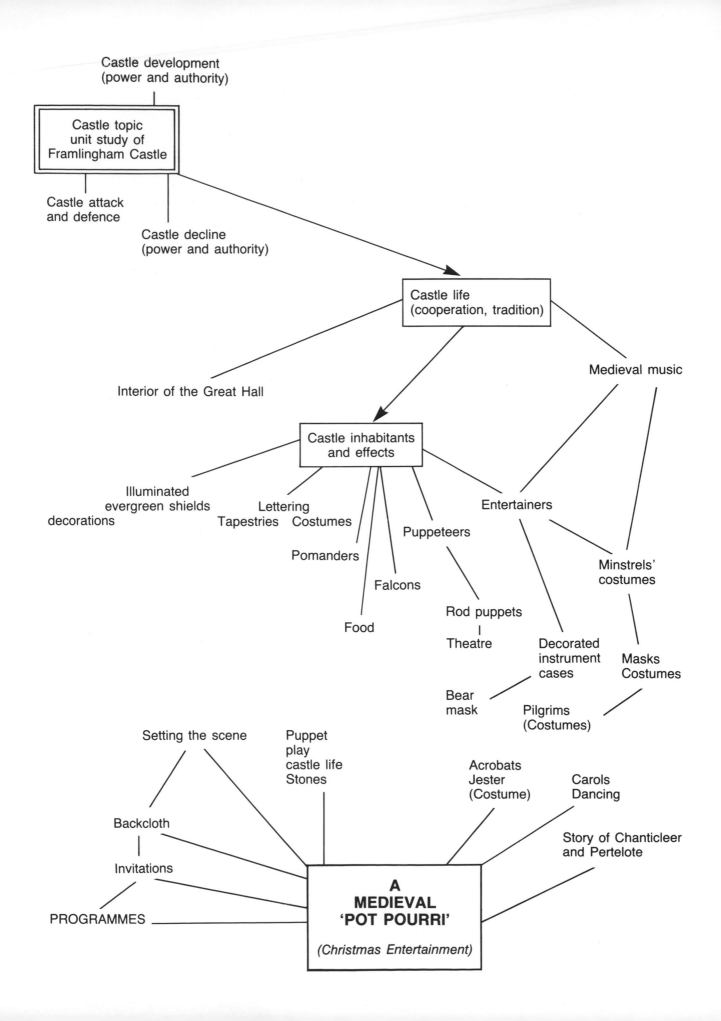

STAGE 4

Designing an Invitation (Junior class)
Challenge and discussion: How could we design an invitation that would create interest and impact to the recipient?
Activities: Individual designs drawn and displayed. The most popular was put on a stencil and duplicated for distribution.

STAGE 5

Performance
All the components came together in the actual performance, with the addition of a special Castle visitor to create the final visual effect:– a friend of the school – an Irish Wolfhound wearing a tunic with a suitable appliqued motif!

The audience consisted of playgroup children and leaders, parents and friends from the village, and Old Age Pensioners.

Photograph by permission of Express Series. (Diss).

Using artists and craftsmen (primary school)

Using artists and craftsmen is a natural extension of using artefacts in schools, or perhaps it should come first?

Most children have no idea of the skills, the organisation, the preliminary skirmishes and the sheer labour which can go into a work of art. Not only are they unused to considering original work, if they see it at all, they probably associate it largely with institutions. It might help children to appreciate that a painting can be as stimulating to live with as a poster of a pop-group, if we popularised our artists a little. I certainly did not understand sculpture until I worked at it myself and, what is more important, worked alongside very interesting people making very interesting structures based upon experience and observation.

I can recount a number of instances where a practising artist or craftsman has worked alongside children, or where children have visited studios or workshops and returned to school to immediate action.

I used a potter on many occasions whilst living and working with the British Army Community in Antwerp. Jos Verhoeven made simple functional containers similar to those made for Flemish homes for centuries. He worked in a badly lit, ancient lean-to building surrounded by his clays, slips and glazes, rows of pots, jugs and jars above his head drying on planks lodged across the roof beams. A huge solid fuel fired kiln dominated the room.

Children watched him throw large crocks in a very short time, his strong fingers easing handles into place before lifting the vessel aside, patting it into shape, and slapping another lump of clay onto the wheel.

We took some of his clay, shovelled from a sack-covered heap on the floor, and returned to school. Some children experimented with our kick wheel, very quickly discovering they did not possess Jos Verhoeven's skill. Some persevered and achieved some sort of pot. Others preferred to build pots by hand and produced quite startling models of the potter at work.

Our interest in clay, as a result of the visit, led us to arrange a trip to a pit where we dug our own clay, processed it ourselves and modelled it into figures and pots which were fired in our own sawdust kiln.

A similar visit to a stonemason, following a trip to an open air exhibition of sculpture, led to experiments with the traditional tools of a stonemason, and eventually, the compromise carving of soft building blocks with rasps and surform tools.

Here in Suffolk, two illustrators have worked in school alongside classes. Christina Newns, who illustrated the Lavenham guide, showed children how she used ink and wash for her drawings of buildings. We have similar buildings in Hadleigh, and her style struck a chord with many children who surprised themselves and each other with their own handling of the medium. Sustained observational drawing became commonplace over the following month.

Brian Edwards, an effervescent comic-strip artist and book illustrator from Bildeston, brought some of his publications to school and worked in front of the children. This exercise was designed to focus attention on imaginative illustration of stories, and certainly fired the imaginations of the most unlikely children, their long stories becoming profusely illustrated.

Perhaps the most influential visit was from Denzil Reeves, the calligrapher and illustrator who lives in Raydon. He came at my invitation to introduce the idea of fine handwriting to the school. His firm, consistent quill pen strokes impressed many children (and staff), and two pieces of his work grace the walls of our school, reminding us of the standards to which we aspire. We now teach a semi-italic style to all children, with varying degrees of success. Some very well formed handwriting is to be found.

More recently, and as a direct result of purchasing two original prints from the Art for Schools exhibition in Gainsborough's Home, Sudbury, we hit on the idea of inviting artists to help us create a gallery of different interpretations of the same subject – our school buildings. The first to accept was Keith Pilling, who draws for the *East Anglian Daily Times* (each Saturday). He spent most of a day completing his picture of our school to the fascination of the children. It will be used for the newspaper, then hung in our school.

I often use the Victorian section of our buildings as a subject, and I anticipate renewed interest in the idea when we have a small gallery as a starting point.

All these visits serve the same end. To bring us close to skill and talent, to help children appreciate the need for sustained concentration, and to develop the appreciation of the value of observational drawing and painting as a means of recording information and experiences.

Bibliography

ADAMS, E. & WARD, C.	Art & the Built Environment	Longman (for Schools Council)	1982
ARNHEIM, R.	Art & Visual Perception	Faber	1967
ART ADVISERS ASSOCIATION	Learning through Drawing	A.A.A. North Eastern Region	1978
BARRETT, M.	Art Education, A Strategy of Course Design.	Heinemann Education Books	1980
BINYON, H.	Puppetry Today	Studio Vista	1966
BOWDEN J.	Using Pictures with Children	Art Advisers Association	1985
CALOUSTE GULBENKIAN FOUNDATION	The Arts in Schools	Calouste Gulbenkian Foundation	1982
CLEMENT R.	The Art Teachers Handbook	Hutchinson	1985
COTTON, A. & HADDON, F.	Learning & Teaching through Art & Craft	Batsford	1974
D.E.S.	Art in Junior Education	H.M.S.O.	1978
D.E.S.	Primary Education in England	H.M.S.O.	1978
DONALDSON, M.	Children's Minds	Faber/Collins	1978
EDWARDS, B.	Drawing on the Right Side of the Brain	Souvenir Press	1981
EHRENZWEIG, A.	The Hidden Order of Art	Paladin	1973
EISNER, E.	Educating Artistic Vision	Collier-Macmillan	1972
FIELD, D.	Change in Art Education	Routledge Kegan Paul	1970
GARDNER, H.	Artful Scribbles	Jill Norman Ltd.	1980
GENTLE, K.	Children and Art Teaching	Croom Helm	1985
GOODNOW. J.	Children's Drawings	Fontana/Open Books	1977
HEREFORD & WORCESTER EDUCATION AUTHORITY	Art for Starters	Hereford & Worcester County Council	1980
HERTFORDSHIRE ADVISORY SERVICE	Primary Art	Hertfordshire County Council	
I.L.E.A.	Drawing on Location	I.L.E.A.: Teachers Art Centre	
I.L.E.A.	Primary Printmaking	I.L.E.A.: Teachers Art Centre	
I.L.E.A.	Childs Play to Initial Art & Craft	I.L.E.A.: Teachers Art Centre	
NEWLAND, Mary and RUBENS, Maurice	Some Functions of Art in the Primary School	I.L.E.A.: Teachers Art Centre	1984
JAMESON, K., & KIDD, P.	Pre School Play	Studio	1974
JAMESON, K.	Junior School Art	Studio	1968
JENNINGS, S.	Art Activity in the Primary School	Heinemann Education	1983
LEICESTER EDUCATION COMMITTEE	Learning through Art in the Primary School.	Leicester County Council	1982
KELLOGG, R.	Analysing Childrens' Art	National Press Books PALO ALTO, California	1972
LAXTON, M.	Using Constructional Materials	Schools Council 8–13 project Van Nostrand Reinhard	1974
LOWENFELD, V.T. Britten, W.	Creative & Mental Growth	Collier Macmillan	1975
MARCOUSE, R.	Using Objects. Schools Council 8–13 project	Van Nostrand Reinhold	1974
MARSHALL, S.	An Experiment in Education	C.U.P.	1963
MENUHIN, Y.	Theme & Variations	Heinemann	1972
MORRIS, D.	The Biology of Art	Methuen	1962
PAINE, S., (editor)	Six Children Draw	Academic Press	1981

Author	Title	Publisher	Year
PICKERING, J.	Visual Education in the Primary School	Batsford Educational	1971
PITFIELD, N.	Drawing	Batsford Educational	1981
PLASKOW, D.	Children & Creative Activity	S.E.A.	1964
ROBERTS, D.	Teaching Art	Batsford	1978
ROBERTSON, S.	Using Natural Objects Schools Council Project 8–13	Van Nostrand Reinhold	1974
READ, H.	Education through Art	Faber & Faber	1959
SCHOOLS COUNCIL	Art 7–11, Occasional Bulletin	Schools Council	1978
SCHOOLS COUNCIL	Resources for Visual Education 7–13	Schools Council	1981
	Critical Studies in Art Education, 1 & 2	Schools Council	1982 & 83
SCIENCE 5–13 PROJECT	Working with Wood		
	Coloured Things		
	Units		
	Holes, Gaps & Cavities		
	Trees		
	Minibeasts	Macdonald Educational	1972, 3 & 4
SPARKES, R.	Exploring Materials with young children	Batsford Macdonald	1975
STAFFORDSHIRE EDUCATION COMMITTEE	Guidelines Art & Craft 5–13		
TAYLOR R.	Educating for Art	Longman	1986
BBC TELEVISION FOR SCHOOLS	Look, Look & Look Again series		1981
HEALTH & SAFETY			
D.E.S.	Safety in Practical Studies	Reprint	1982
INSTITUTE OF CERAMICS	Health & Safety in Ceramics	Available from The Institute of Ceramics, Federation House, Station Road, Stoke on Trent. ST4 2RT.	